OUTDOOR ENCYCLOPEDIAS

THE HUNTING ENCYCLOPEDIA

BY KATE CONLEY

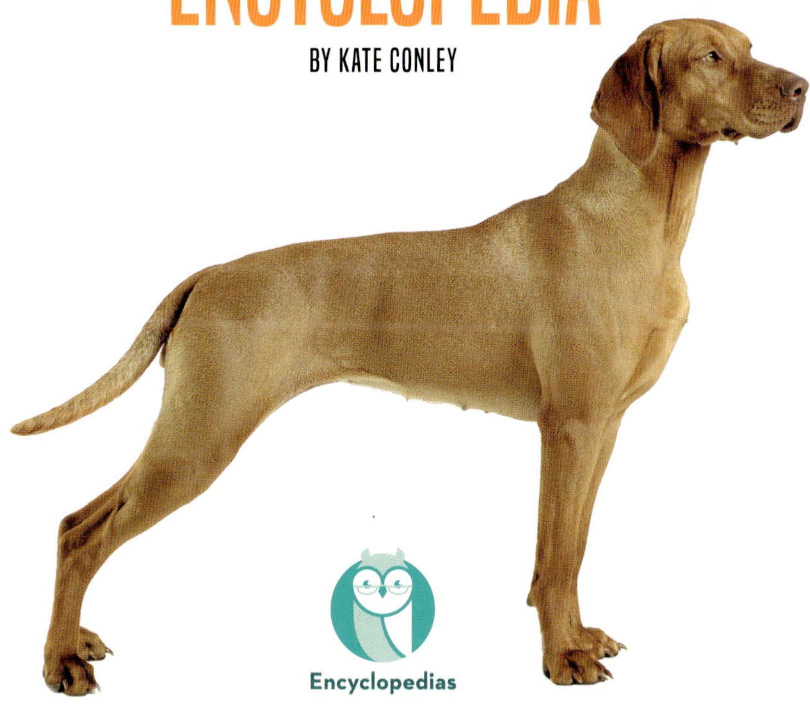

Encyclopedias

An Imprint of Abdo Reference

abdobooks.com

TABLE OF CONTENTS

THE HUNTING TRADITION

Hunting requires skill, patience, and a bit of luck.

Every year, about 11.5 million Americans head to the nation's forests, fields, and wetlands to hunt. They are continuing a tradition that is thousands of years old. Learning to hunt is a rite of passage for many people. The thrill of a successful hunt is what draws hunters to the sport year after year.

While hunting is considered a sport today, that has not always been the case. Along with gathering wild plants, hunting was an essential source of food for most of human history. Early hunters used simple weapons found in nature. With stones, hunters could take down birds and other small game. Sharpened sticks allowed hunters to kill larger animals at a distance.

People began to grow crops about 10,000 years ago. Later, they domesticated livestock. These practices gave people more control over their food sources. But hunting remained important for survival.

A panel from Assyria dating to the 600s BCE shows people hunting lions with spears.

Over time, the weapons hunters used became more advanced. By 5000 BCE, people in Egypt and the Middle Eastern nations of Assyria and Persia began to use bows and arrows for hunting. They provided greater accuracy, power, and range than earlier throwing weapons.

A textile from the 600s CE depicts bowhunting.

HUNTING AS SPORT

As the practices of farming and raising livestock advanced, people relied less on hunting. Some people still needed to hunt for survival, but for others it became a sport. Rulers and members of the upper class hunted for pleasure rather than survival. Between 1000 and 1500 CE, special hunting grounds were set aside in parts of Europe and Asia. Only wealthy, powerful people could hunt in them legally. Anyone caught illegally hunting in these grounds faced severe punishments, including death.

The harquebus was a type of firearm developed in Spain in the 1500s.

The development of gunpowder and firearms began in China in the 1100s. By the 1500s, people were using them to hunt in parts of Asia and Europe. Early firearms could be dangerous and unpredictable. But they increased the efficiency of a hunt. They allowed hunters to kill more game with less effort than at any time in the past.

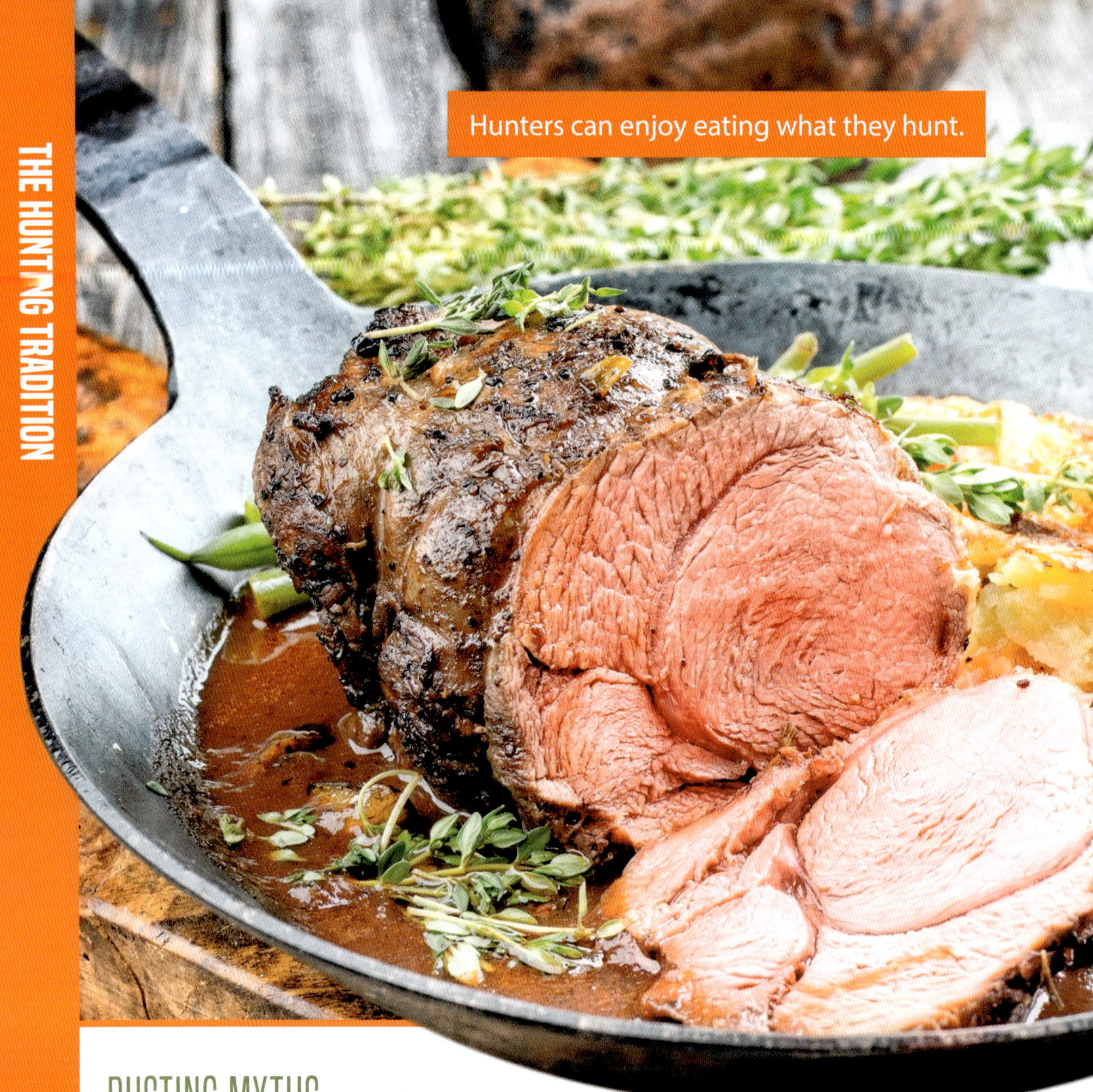

Hunters can enjoy eating what they hunt.

BUSTING MYTHS

Some people around the world still rely on hunting for food. But in other places, such as the United States, many hunters do not need to hunt. They do it for fun. The rise in hunting for sport has led to changes in hunting. Regulations have increased to protect species populations. And human safety awareness has also grown.

Although hunting involves dangerous tools, increasing safety has been a key focus since the 1950s. At that time, some of the first hunter safety courses began. They provided instruction in how to handle firearms and follow safe hunting practices in the field. As these classes spread across the nation, hunting accidents and injuries decreased. For example, in the state of Minnesota, nine years between 1960 and 1975 had more than 100 hunting accidents. Ten of those years had ten or more fatalities. There were fewer than 33,000 hunting licenses issued for each recorded year in that period. By comparison, between 2005 and 2020, there wasn't a single year with more than 26 accidents, and deaths ranged from zero to four. There were more than 475,000 licenses issued each of these years, with most years selling more than 800,000 licenses.

Thanks to education programs, injuries while hunting are rare.

By 2020, women were the fastest-growing group of hunters. Since 2006, the number of women who hunt had risen by 25 percent. That translates to more than one million women out in the fields hunting.

Women have been hunting for all of human history.

Hunters enjoy being in nature.

REASONS FOR HUNTING

Hunters make up about 5 percent of the US population. The reasons they take to the field vary widely. For many, hunting provides an opportunity to spend time outdoors. It is a chance to unplug from technology and step away from the busyness of daily life. Hunting puts people in touch with nature, allowing them to observe wildlife. They develop a keen awareness of scents, sounds, and scenery while tracking game.

DID YOU KNOW?

In the United States and Canada, 89 percent of hunters are male and 11 percent are female. Half of all hunters are over the age of 45. By ethnicity, 94 percent of hunters are white, while 3 percent are Black and 3 percent are other ethnicities.

Hunters can know that the meat they eat came from animals that led natural lives in the wild.

Other hunters value the sense of self-reliance they get from the sport. Buying meat from the grocery store is easier and cheaper than hunting for one's own meat. But cost and convenience are not why many hunters head to the field. Instead, for them it's about personal satisfaction. They like knowing that they have used their own skills to harvest the game they put on their tables.

Conservation also motivates many hunters. Biologists keep track of wildlife populations. If one game population is starting to get too large, it can cause problems. It can upset the balance of an ecosystem. It can also cause unwanted interactions between wildlife and humans. Biologists rely on hunters to reduce populations that have grown too large. This keeps the game populations healthy for the future.

Hunters typically want to ensure game populations remain steady for future generations.

For many, hunting is a way to carry on tradition. Some families have been hunting together for generations. Planning a hunt, scouting a site, and tracking game provide families with quality time together. Field skills and knowledge are often passed down from older to younger generations. Hunting also provides insights into the ways of life of earlier generations.

Parents who hunt will often take their kids with them.

Hunters must follow laws to protect people and the animal populations.

Hunting is a privilege afforded to all citizens in the United States. In other parts of the world, only wealthy and powerful people who own land are allowed to hunt. But in the United States, the wildlife belongs to all citizens. To ensure hunting remains available, the US government balances the desire to hunt with conservation of the country's abundant wildlife.

GAME

It's important for hunters to know the difference between species and between males and females within a species so they can follow harvesting laws.

One of the many skills a hunter must learn is how to identify game. Game is any animal that can be hunted legally. Sometimes hunting laws permit shooting only a male animal or an animal that is fully grown. Other times, two species of game may look similar, but only one is legal to hunt. In these situations, identifying game is important. Identifying game helps a hunter follow the law and conserve game for future generations.

GAME BIRDS

Game is often divided into the following broad categories: game birds, small game, and big game. Game birds include many species of wild birds. Waterfowl is one category of game birds. Waterfowl live near ponds, lakes, and rivers. Geese and ducks are commonly hunted types of waterfowl. Upland game birds include grouse, quails, pheasants, and wild turkeys.

Hunters enjoy the challenge of shooting a bird in flight.

Geese have long necks and sturdy bodies. They have short legs, webbed feet, and flat bills. Geese can vary greatly in size depending on the species. A Canada goose can reach up to 20 pounds (9 kg), while a Ross's goose averages only 3 to 4 pounds (1.4 to 1.8 kg). Geese may be gray, white, or brown in color.

Geese often fly in a V-shaped formation when migrating.

Geese are hunted for their meat and soft down feathers.

All geese are migratory birds. They fly south in the fall and north in the spring. Their long, pointed wings allow them to fly great distances. Some species can fly up to 1,000 miles (1,600 km) without stopping. They nest in fields and grassy areas near fresh water.

Canada geese and snow geese are two commonly hunted species. In North America, 2.6 million Canada geese are hunted each year. The goose hunting season is from late summer into early winter, and spring, though dates vary by state.

Male mallards are known for their iridescent green heads.

Ducks are another type of waterfowl. Ducks have short necks, large bills, webbed feet, and plump bodies. Wild ducks can range in size from 2 to 4 pounds (0.9 to 1.8 kg). Their feathers are waterproof, and the coloring of the feathers varies by species. Duck hunting season is in the fall and early winter. Many people enjoy hunting ducks for the meat.

Ducks are commonly divided into two types: puddle ducks and diving ducks. Puddle ducks live in shallow waters. Their tails tip up in the air as they dip their heads below the water in search of food. Mallards, teals, and pintails are common types of puddle ducks. Diving ducks live in deep waters. They find food while diving and swimming underwater for long periods. Canvasbacks, redheads, and ringnecks are common types of diving ducks.

Grouse, quails, and pheasants are all small-bodied wild game birds. The hunting season for these birds varies by state, but it commonly runs from the fall through early winter. Hunters like these types of game birds because they are challenging to hunt. They also provide delicious meat.

Ruffed grouse live in forests.

Grouse are similar in size and appearance to chickens. Ruffed grouse are the most common grouse species in North America. They are also one of the most popular game birds to hunt. Ruffed grouse have brown feathers and a fan-shaped tail.

Quails are another type of wild game bird. Quails are small, usually growing to between 8 and 12 inches (20 and 30 cm) long. Their feathers are patterned in shades of rust, brown, gray, and cream. They live in areas with tall grasses and brush, which provide shelter.

The most common species of quail in North America is the bobwhite.

In most states, it is legal to hunt only male pheasants, *pictured*.

Pheasants are known for their long, beautiful tail feathers. The ring-necked pheasant is a popular species to hunt. It is between 20 and 36 inches (51 and 91 cm) long. Bright-red feathers encircle the ring-neck's eyes. A white stripe on its neck gives way to a patterned brown body. Pheasants live in grasslands and farm fields.

Turkeys live in groups called flocks.

Wild turkeys are large game birds that are native to North America. They can grow to 3 feet (0.9 m) in length and weigh up to 25 pounds (11 kg). A turkey's head has reddish, bumpy skin. A wattle extends from the throat. The wattle is a long, loose piece of skin. Dark-brown, black, and gray feathers cover a turkey's body. Males have large tails shaped like fans.

Wooded areas near fresh water are common places for turkeys to live. They also live near grain fields that have been freshly harvested. Turkey hunting has two seasons. One is in the spring, and the other is in the fall. Turkeys are hunted for their plentiful meat.

SMALL GAME

Small game species are generally animals that weigh less than 40 pounds (18 kg). They come from a variety of animal families including rabbits, rodents, weasels, wild dogs, and wild cats. Small game is often hunted or trapped for its fur and meat.

Hunters who shoot turkeys can share their meat with family and friends for a traditional Thanksgiving meal.

Wild rabbits in North America are part of a group known as cottontails, which includes several species. They get this name from the white fur on the undersides of their tails. Their bellies, chins, and inner legs are also white. The heads, backs, and ears of cottontails range in color from brown to gray.

Rabbits have sharp eyesight, and their large ears give them excellent hearing. At full size, they average 1 to 1.3 feet (0.3 to 0.4 m) in length and weigh 2 to 3 pounds (0.9 to 1.4 kg). Rabbits live in areas with thick brush cover, which provides protection from predators. Hunting season for rabbits commonly runs from the fall through late winter. Hunters seek out rabbits for their nutritious meat and soft fur.

People can hunt different types of animals at once, such as rabbits, ducks, and pheasants.

Squirrels are often hunted for food. Licenses to hunt squirrels are relatively inexpensive.

Some animals in the rodent family are commonly hunted. These animals include squirrels, prairie dogs, woodchucks, and muskrats. Rodents are mammals with long, sharp teeth that never stop growing. They gnaw on objects to keep their teeth from growing too long. Some rodents are sought after for their soft pelts, which are sometimes used to make clothing.

The fox squirrel is North America's largest native tree squirrel.

Squirrels have long bodies with long, fluffy tails. They spend a lot of time in trees. In North America, the eastern gray squirrel and the eastern fox squirrel are common. Squirrels average 8 to 10 inches (20 to 25 cm) in length and weigh approximately 1.5 pounds (0.7 kg). They are generally gray and brown in color. Squirrels are usually hunted in the fall and winter, and people eat the meat.

Prairie dogs are burrowing rodents. They have tan-colored fur, short legs, sturdy bodies, and sharp claws. Prairie dogs live in large groups called towns. A town can include up to 50 burrows and 500 residents. They dig their burrows in prairies, grasslands, and fields. Fully grown prairie dogs are 9 to 15 inches (23 to 38 cm) long and weigh between 1 and 3 pounds (0.5 and 1.4 kg).

SEEKING OUT PRAIRIE DOGS

Prairie dogs are difficult to hunt because they are small and move quickly. For this reason, some hunters seek out prairie dogs to improve their shooting skills. Farmers may hire hunters to shoot prairie dogs because these animals can damage farm fields. In most states, prairie dogs can be hunted all year.

The black-tailed prairie dog is one species of prairie dog that can be hunted.

Woodchucks are another type of burrowing rodent. They have rounded bodies, short legs, and bushy tails. Most woodchucks are brown or gray in color, and they can grow quite large. An adult may be up to 1.7 feet (0.5 m) long and weigh 13 pounds (6 kg). They live along the edges of forests, prairies, and fields. Both prairie dog and woodchuck burrows can damage farm fields. This is the main reason they are hunted.

Woodchucks are also called groundhogs.

The American mink lives close to water.

Weasels are a family of animals with long, slender bodies and short legs. Members of this family include badgers, ferrets, minks, martens, and fishers. These animals are known as furbearers, which means they are typically hunted for their pelts. Animals in the weasel family are often hunted using traps. These animals live in a variety of habitats, though they usually make their dens under rocks or in burrows. They are small, quick, agile animals that can be difficult to catch.

Coyotes are a type of wild dog. They have thick, coarse fur that is usually buff or reddish-brown in color. Coyotes have long, bushy tails and tall, pointed ears. They can grow up to 2 feet (0.6 m) tall at the shoulder and weigh between 20 and 50 pounds (9 and 23 kg). These wild dogs are fast and can run at speeds of up to 40 miles per hour (64 kmh). They live in a wide variety of settings, from urban areas to prairies.

Coyotes live in many different habitats, from hot deserts to cold, snowy climates.

Coyotes are hunted as pests near farms and ranches because they can kill livestock.

The hunting season for coyotes varies by state, but it is usually in the winter. Coyotes are often hunted for their fur, and they have their thickest coats in the winter months. Sometimes coyotes are also hunted because their populations grow too large. They have few natural predators, so hunters help keep the population in balance.

Hunters should know the difference between Canadian lynx, *pictured*, and bobcats so they don't accidentally shoot a lynx.

Lynx are a group of medium-sized wild cats. The only type of lynx that can be hunted legally is the bobcat. Laws in nearly all states protect other lynx from being hunted. Adult bobcats can weigh up to 26 pounds (12 kg) and reach 2.8 feet (0.9 m) in length. Their fur may be buff, reddish-brown, or gray. Bobcats have short tails with black tips, and their ears have short tufts of hair on them. They are nocturnal animals that live in wooded areas.

Bobcats are furbearers. Their pelts are some of the most valuable ones on the market. Often bobcat pelts are used to make fur coats. The bobcat hunting season varies by state. It generally runs from late fall through late winter. Most bobcats are trapped rather than shot to avoid damaging the pelts.

Bobcats have smaller feet and shorter legs than Canadian lynx.

BIG GAME

Big game species are the largest animals that hunters can seek. In the United States, these animals include deer, moose, elk, caribou, bears, and wild hogs. People hunt big game for the meat. Big game can sometimes take several days to find. People enjoy putting their skills to the test and the thrill of taking down an animal much bigger than themselves.

People can book game-hunting trips with guides to try to take down large game.

Hunters may decorate their homes with the animals they hunt.

Hunting bears is legal in several states, including Alaska, New York, Maine, Vermont, Massachusetts, New Hampshire, and New Jersey. Bear hunting season typically runs from late summer through late fall, though dates vary by state. When the weather becomes cold, bears hibernate in caves or dens. Bears are typically sought after for the challenge they provide to hunters as well as for their meat. Hunted species in the United States include the black bear and the brown bear.

Bears have more bone and fat protecting their organs than other game animals, such as deer. This makes it harder to get a clean shot.

Black bears have black fur, though they may also be brown or even white in color. They typically eat plants, berries, and fish. However, black bears are not terribly picky, so hunters must take care not to leave food or garbage lying around. Adult males can grow as large as 6 feet (1.8 m) long and weigh up to 400 pounds (180 kg). Despite their large size, black bears can climb trees.

Brown bears, called grizzly bears in North America, are even larger than black bears. An adult male can grow to 8 feet (2.4 m) long and weigh more than 1,000 pounds (450 kg). These bears typically have brown fur and are easily recognized by the hump in between their shoulders. These powerful animals have long, sharp claws, which make them excellent at digging. Laws heavily restrict the hunting of brown bears. Alaska is the only state where it is legal.

Mammals with antlers and hooves are some of the most commonly hunted game. Animals from the deer family are especially popular in North America. The hunting season for these animals is usually in the fall. They are often hunted for the challenge, as well as for the meat they provide to hunters.

The brown bear is classified as threatened in most US states.

White-tailed deer have brown coats in the summer, grayish coats in the winter, and white bellies year-round. These deer stand between 2.5 and 3.3 feet (0.8 and 1 m) tall from hoof to shoulder. They can weigh anywhere from 100 to 300 pounds (45 to 140 kg). Male deer are called bucks. They are usually larger and have antlers. Female deer are called does. They are smaller and do not have antlers.

White-tailed deer

Caribou

Elk

Caribou are deer that are much larger than white-tailed deer. They stand between 4 and 5 feet (1.2 and 1.5 m) at the shoulder and weigh up to 700 pounds (320 kg). Caribou live in the forests of Alaska, Idaho, Washington, and parts of Canada. They have thick coats that are usually brown or gray. Caribou live in herds and migrate thousands of miles during the summer and winter seasons.

DID YOU KNOW?

White-tailed deer are the continent's most widely hunted big game species. They also have the largest population of any big game species in North America.

Like caribou, elk are large deer. Male elk are called bulls, and they often grow to be 5 feet (1.5 m) tall from hoof to shoulder. Bulls weigh up to 1,000 pounds (450 kg) and have massive antlers that can span 5 feet (1.5 m). Elk typically have reddish-brown bodies, tan rumps, and brown necks.

Moose can be found near bodies of fresh water, where they browse on aquatic vegetation in addition to plants on land.

Moose are the largest members of the deer family. They live in cool, northern climates such as Canada and Alaska. Moose have long legs, broad shoulders, and massive bodies. They can stand up to 7.5 feet (2.3 m) tall at the shoulder and weigh up to 1,800 pounds (820 kg). The most defining feature of a male moose is its antlers. Moose antlers can be massive, spanning 6 feet (1.8 m) and weighing 85 pounds (39 kg).

Wild hogs are another large mammal that hunters seek. In the United States, wild hogs are the offspring of escaped domestic pigs and Eurasian boars, and they are not native to the continent. Adult males can weigh up to 400 pounds (180 kg). Wild pigs are smart and adapt to their surroundings easily. They dig for food, which damages land and property. Hunting wild hogs is not legal in every state.

Wild hogs reproduce quickly and have few predators in the United States, making their populations difficult to control.

GEAR

Hunting involves spending many hours outside, so dressing for the weather is important. Being cold and wet can make hunting miserable or even dangerous. Experienced hunters know this, and they choose clothing that will protect them from the elements. This will vary depending on where a person is hunting, as well as the season. The clothing should also be comfortable and allow for easy movement.

It's important that hunters be prepared for the temperature, wearing clothing that will protect their bodies for extended periods of time outdoors.

Wearing layers while hunting is a smart option. A base layer is a pair of pants and a shirt that fit snugly to a person's body. Its purpose is to provide warmth and to wick sweat or water away from the body. Staying dry will keep the hunter warm. The base layer is typically made from merino wool or a synthetic fabric such as polyester. Base layers can be purchased in different weights depending on what temperatures a hunter will be exposed to in the field.

Thermal underwear is another name for the base layer.

Hunters in southern regions where it stays warm may not need as many layers as hunters in the north.

The middle layer goes over the base layer. Pants and shirts for this layer should be loose but not baggy to work most efficiently. This layer's job is to act as insulation, trapping heat next to the hunter's body. Middle layers are often made of fleece, polyester, down, or wool. Sometimes hunters wear more than one middle layer depending on the weather.

BLEND IN AND STAND OUT

One consideration for choosing an outer layer is color. Some hunters prefer to wear outer layers that have a camouflage pattern. This keeps them hidden from the game they are hunting. Solid earth tones such as brown, green, tan, or gray also work for this purpose. Many states require a hunter to wear blaze orange or blaze pink on the upper body. This is a safety measure. The bright color draws attention, preventing other hunters from mistaking the person as game.

The outer layer acts as a shield to protect the inner layers. It includes a pair of pants and a jacket that resist rain and wind. The material should resist rips and snags from branches and underbrush. A hunter should also consider how much noise the outer layer makes when moving. If it is too noisy, it might scare away the game.

It's especially important to wear wind-resistant clothing when hunting in open fields with little to block the wind.

FEET, HANDS, AND HEAD

Hunters must also think about how to keep their feet, hands, and head warm. Having warm, dry, properly fitting boots is important to make the hunt comfortable. A good pair of hunting boots has rugged traction on the soles, is waterproof, and is well insulated. Hunting boots can be made of leather or synthetic materials.

Hunters who spend a lot of time in wet, marshy areas may choose to wear rubber boots.

Wool socks made for outdoor activities can be purchased from outdoor recreation stores.

When trying on boots, hunters should wear the socks they plan to use while in the field. This will ensure the best fit. Much like base layers, outdoor socks come in different weights. Hunters should choose the weight of their socks based on the weather. The cooler the temperature, the heavier weight the sock should be. Hunting socks are commonly made from merino wool or synthetic blends such as polyester and nylon.

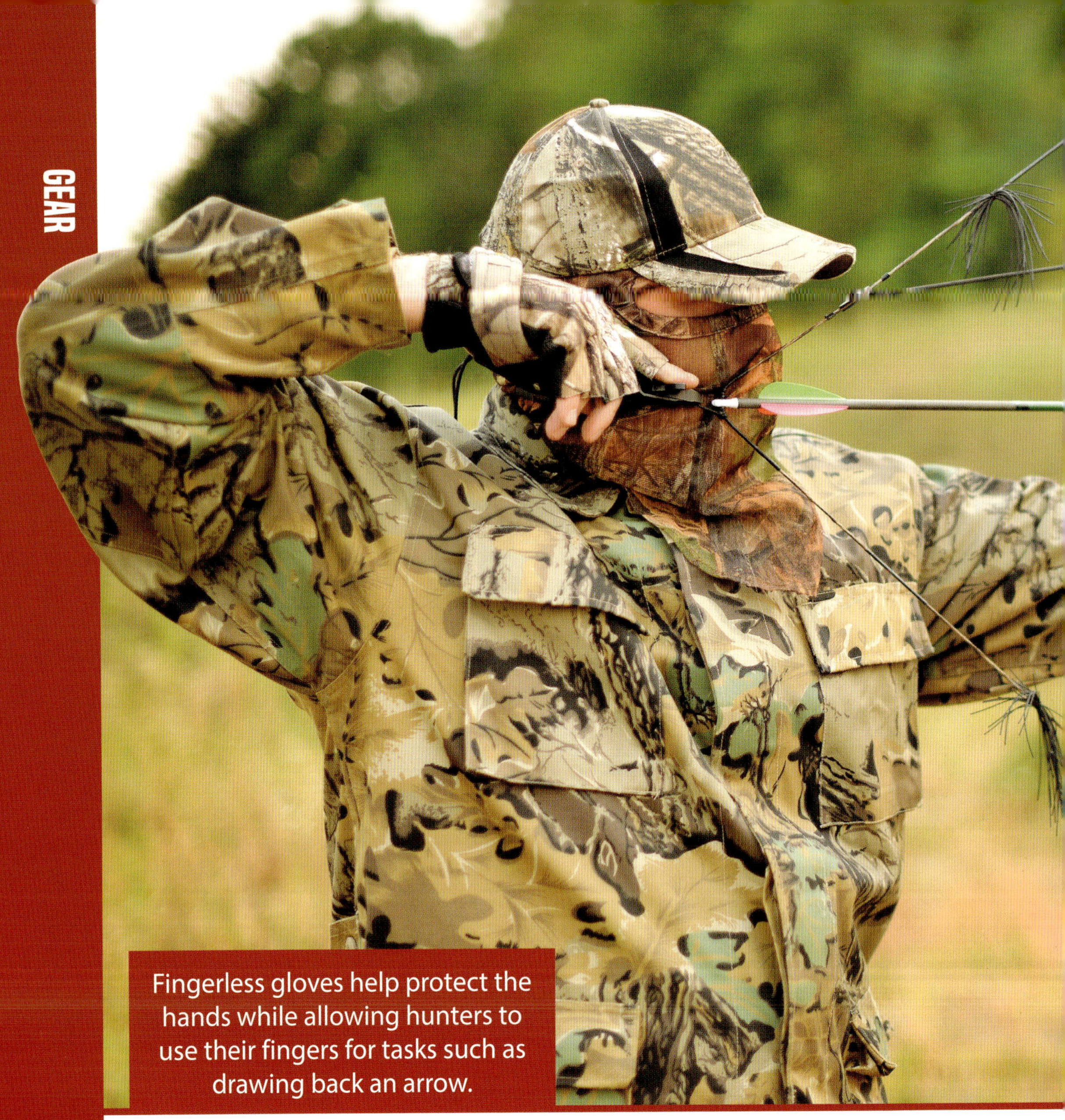

Fingerless gloves help protect the hands while allowing hunters to use their fingers for tasks such as drawing back an arrow.

A good pair of gloves is another essential piece of hunting gear. Not only will gloves keep fingers warm on cold days, but they will also protect against cuts and scrapes while in the field. Fingerless gloves are a popular option on days that aren't very cold. They allow a hunter full range of motion with his or her fingers. This makes shooting a firearm or bow and arrow easier. Full-fingered gloves offer more warmth and protection, but they limit the fingers' full range of motion.

The warmest option for a hunter's hands is a heavy-duty pair of mittens. However, they greatly limit the fingers' movements. A hunter will often wear a thin pair of gloves inside the mittens. When the hunter needs to shoot, he or she can quickly take off the mittens while still keeping his or her hands warm.

Wearing glove liners inside mittens provides the most warmth while also preventing heat loss when the hunter has to remove the mittens.

Hats are also essential when hunting. In mild weather, a hunter may choose a baseball-style cap or any wide-brimmed hat. These can protect a hunter from rain or bright sun, but they provide little warmth. Lightweight beanies or stocking caps can keep hunters warm on cool days. When temperatures dip even lower, hunters often turn to warmer hats. Fur-lined hats with ear flaps can keep a hunter comfortable in the coldest weather. A hunter may also wear a neck gaiter. This is a loop of cloth pulled over the head that sits around the neck.

Some hunters wear balaclavas, which are a hat and neck gaiter in one.

Some decoys are made to float in water.

DECOYS, GAME CALLS, AND BINOCULARS

Hunting waterfowl requires specialized gear. Many hunters like to use confidence decoys. These are models made to look like different kinds of birds. The decoys act as a signal to the real birds that an area is safe. When a hunter places the decoys in a body of water, other birds may land near them, giving the hunter a chance to take a shot.

Decoys can be used on land as well as in the water.

Decoys can look very realistic. For example, a set of mallard decoys may display a variety of duck behaviors. Some decoys may have their heads up, looking relaxed and calm. Others may tip up with their tails in the air, looking as though they are feeding. Still others may be positioned with their heads facing back as if they are sleeping. When a group of these decoys is floating on the water, it can be a convincing scene.

Like decoys, game calls have the power to draw animals near a hunter. Game calls are devices that mimic the sound of animals. Game calls can be used with many kinds of animals, including turkeys, ducks, geese, moose, and white-tailed deer. Some game calls are purchased at hunting stores. Others can be made with simple supplies found in nature or at home. For example, squirrel hunters may click together two quarters. It creates sounds like those made by squirrels.

Game calls attract animals by using sounds such as mating calls.

Being able to see the game they've drawn near is important for hunters. Many carry binoculars as part of their gear. Binoculars provide valuable information to hunters. In many states, laws determine what species, sex, and age of game can be hunted and when. Binoculars give hunters this key information before they shoot. When pursuing game, hunters can also use binoculars to assess challenging terrain. This lets them locate the most efficient and safest paths.

Binoculars help hunters ensure they shoot the species of animal they mean to shoot.

Binoculars can be useful for identifying the best spot to cross a stream or where there may be rough terrain.

The binoculars hunters use must have a few basic features. They must not get easily damaged in the field. They must be lightweight and small enough to carry easily. And they must have powerful enough magnification to make them useful. Some advanced binoculars also have range finders in them. They can provide an exact distance between the hunter and the game. The distance is usually displayed digitally inside the lens.

Range finders can fit in a pocket easily.

Some hunters use range finders that are separate from binoculars. Range finders have only a single magnifying lens to look through. When game is centered in the lens, a laser can accurately estimate the animal's distance from the hunter. The benefit of range finders over binoculars is that they are generally lighter, smaller, and less expensive.

OTHER GEAR

Hunters must carry the proper game tags for the animals they're hunting. Each state's game tags are a bit different. In general, the tags outline the type of game, the type of weapon, and the dates when the hunt can happen legally. Hunters must have these tags to prove that they have legal permission to hunt the game they seek. After game has been sighted and shot, hunters need to attach the tag to it.

Different states have different rules about where the game tag should be attached.

For people headed to lakes and rivers to hunt waterfowl, a few extra pieces of gear are required. The most important is a life jacket. If a boat capsizes or a hunter falls overboard, a life jacket can be the difference between life and death. Another key piece of gear is a pair of waders. They come in several styles, but chest waders are among the most common. They look a bit like overalls with boots built into them. Waders are made from waterproof fabric, which keeps hunters dry when they slog through mud and cold water.

DID YOU KNOW?

Hunting in the United States is a multibillion-dollar business. In 2016, hunters spent $5.9 billion on firearms, ammunition, and archery equipment; $3.1 billon on food and lodging; $630 million on hunting clothing; and $256 million on licenses and permits.

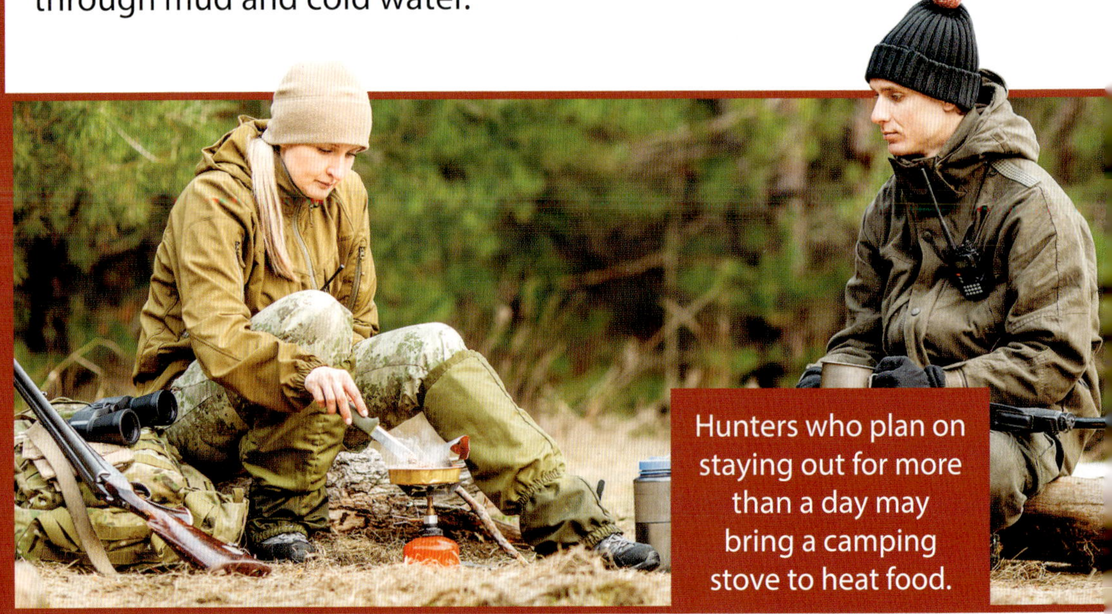

Hunters who plan on staying out for more than a day may bring a camping stove to heat food.

Electronic devices may not always work outdoors, so having a map and compass on hand can help hunters find their way back.

Hunters may need additional gear if they plan to stay in the field for several days without returning home. And even if the hunt is for just a day, unexpected events happen in the field. This means an outdoor survival kit should be a standard item included along with other hunting gear. A map and compass are useful to avoid getting lost in unfamiliar terrain. Other key pieces of gear for a long hunting trip include a small tent, sleeping bags, food, and matches.

FIREARMS, BOWS, AND TRAPS

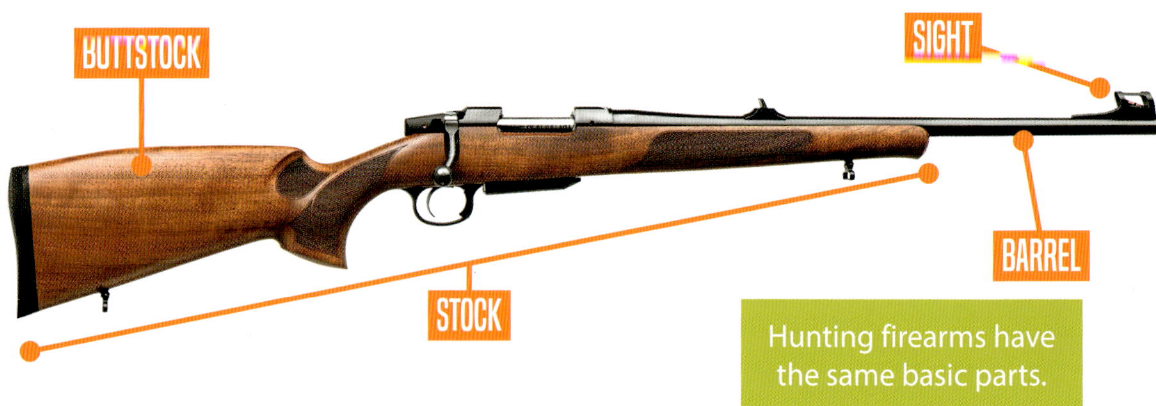

Hunting firearms have the same basic parts.

Hunters have a variety of firearms to choose from when heading to the field. Firearms are devices that use gunpowder. When the gunpower ignites, it projects bullets or shells. The two main types of hunting firearms are shotguns and rifles. Both of these firearms have long barrels attached to a stock. At the end of the stock is the buttstock, which rests against a hunter's shoulder and cheek when shooting. The hunter uses a sight on the barrel to take aim.

The main differences between a shotgun and a rifle are ammunition type and barrel design. Ammunition used in a shotgun is called shot. It is a cartridge that holds small, metal pellets. When the pellets leave the barrel, they spread out in a pattern. This is an advantage when hunting small targets that move quickly. The size of the pellets can vary. Small pellets, which are called bird shot, are used for small game such as birds, rabbits, and squirrels. Large pellets, which are called buckshot, are used for big game such as deer.

There are many small, round projectiles in a shotgun cartridge.

A rifle cartridge has a single bullet at the tip.

In contrast, a rifle shoots a cartridge with a single bullet in it. The barrel of a rifle is specially made for this type of ammunition. Inside the barrel is a spiral pattern called rifling. The bullet follows the path of the rifling, which makes it spin. This increases the bullet's power and accuracy.

Many hunting firearms open between the buttstock and barrel for loading cartridges.

FIREARM ACTION DESIGN

Firearms come in three main action designs: break action, pump action, and semiautomatic. A break action firearm has a hinged section on the barrel, where a hunter loads a cartridge directly into the chamber. A single-barreled firearm holds one cartridge. It must be reloaded every time it is fired. This type of firearm is usually lightweight, inexpensive, and easy to operate.

Some break-action firearms have two barrels. This is more common with shotguns than rifles. A double-barreled firearm holds two cartridges, one in each of its barrels. This allows a hunter to fire twice before reloading. Over-under shotguns have the barrels stacked

Over-under shotgun

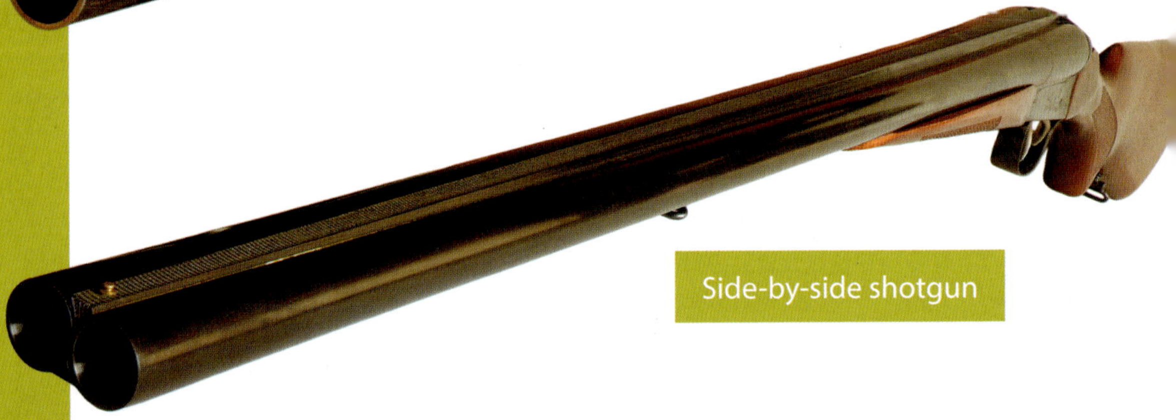

Side-by-side shotgun

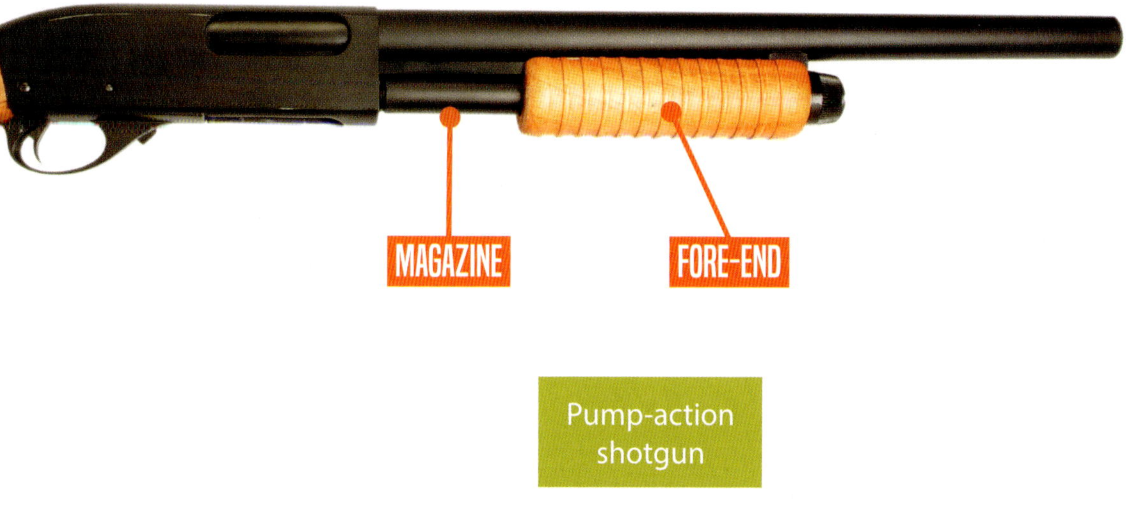

Pump-action shotgun

on top of each other. Side-by-side shotguns have the barrels placed next to each other. Double-barreled shotguns are more expensive than single-barrels, but they are popular among many hunters.

A pump-action firearm has a single barrel, but its design allows hunters to take multiple shots without reloading. A storage tube called a magazine is housed below the barrel. It can hold several cartridges. After taking a shot, the hunter slides the fore-end below the barrel toward the buttstock. This ejects the used cartridge. The hunter then pushes the slider forward, which pushes a new cartridge into the barrel. This allows a hunter to take several shots in a row. It is much faster than having to reload after each shot. The only break between shots is while the hunter is moving the fore-end.

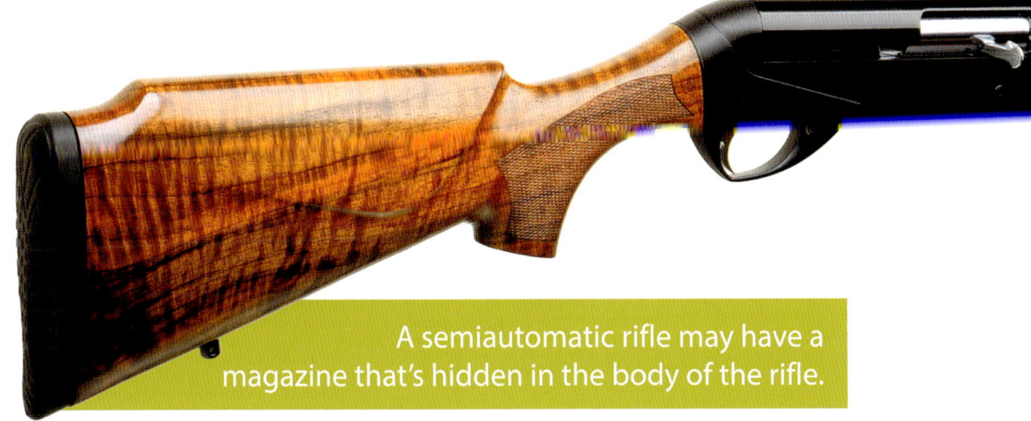

A semiautomatic rifle may have a magazine that's hidden in the body of the rifle.

Much like a pump-action firearm, a semiautomatic allows a hunter to take multiple shots without reloading. But it works a bit differently. Its magazine does not require a hunter to do anything to reload the barrel. Instead, the gas released from firing powers a reloading mechanism in the magazine. This allows hunters to fire rapidly, one shot after another.

Once hunters have chosen a type of firearm, they must find a model that is the proper size and weight. A firearm should be fitted to a hunter's body so that it is comfortable to carry and shoot. If it is too heavy or the recoil is too powerful, the hunter may have trouble controlling

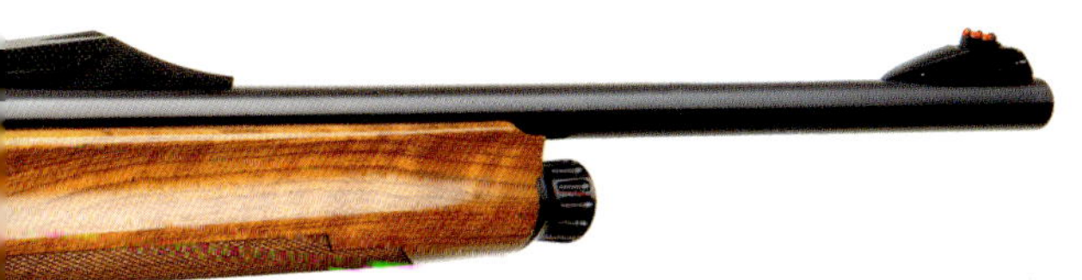

the firearm safely. No matter what type of firearm a hunter chooses, he or she must be trained in how to use it safely. Many cities, counties, and states offer firearms safety classes especially for hunters.

Hunters should practice handling and shooting their firearms before going out to hunt.

The long history of humans using bows and arrows to hunt attracts people to bowhunting.

BOWHUNTING

Firearms can be accurate for targets a few hundred yards away. But using firearms is not the only way to hunt. Some hunters prefer using bows and arrows, which must be shot at a much closer range. Bows and arrows are what people have hunted with for most of human history. Today, bows can be simple or quite advanced. Bows and arrows are made from a variety of materials including wood, aluminum, carbon, or plastic. Bowstrings are typically made of plastic or polyethylene that is wrapped in nylon. Bowhunters have many choices: longbows, recurve bows, compound bows, and crossbows are all hunting options.

Longbows are the simplest type of bow. They are traditionally made of wood with a spot to grip it in the middle. Some hunters choose to use the longbow because it provides a more traditional hunting experience. But the longbow can take years of practice to master, and pulling back the bowstring requires a lot of strength. The longbow's performance is also greatly affected by humidity and weather.

DID YOU KNOW?

Firearms are considerably more popular among hunters than bows and arrows. In the 2022 deer hunting season, 74 percent of hunters used firearms. The remaining 26 percent used archery equipment.

Arrows shot from longbows travel more slowly than arrows shot from other bow types.

Recurve bows are like longbows with a few key differences. They get their name from the tips of the bow, which curve away from the archer. The curved tips provide extra power to the arrow when it is shot. Recurve bows provide more power, speed, and accuracy than longbows. They are also lighter in weight and shorter in length, making them easier to carry in the field. Much like the longbow, recurve bows require a lot of practice to master.

Recurve bows are louder than longbows because the string slaps into the sides of each end when released.

Compound bows were invented in 1966.

Compound bows are a more complex type of bow. They use a system of levers, pulleys, and cables. This system makes them more efficient. A hunter can pull back on the bowstring with less effort. As a result, compound bows can shoot faster and more accurately than traditional bows.

DRAW LENGTH AND DRAW WEIGHT

For traditional bows, a hunter's height and strength determine the right size bow. To find the correct fit, hunters must look at the draw length and the draw weight. Draw length is the length required to pull a bow back fully. It is measured in inches. Draw weight is the amount of force required for a full pull of the drawstring. It is measured in pounds.

Hunters should consider their individual needs when selecting the right type of bow for their purposes.

A crossbow is another type of bow that some hunters use. It is like a compound bow, but it is mounted on a stock and shot in a horizontal position. The stock looks like the body of a rifle or shotgun. To shoot a crossbow, hunters do not have to physically pull a bowstring. Instead, they can use a cocking device to pull it back. Hunters can put hooks on the string on both sides of the stock. Then they use a crank handle to draw the string tight until it clicks into place. To shoot, hunters pull a trigger similar to the ones on a rifle or shotgun.

The benefit of using a crossbow is that the hunter does not have to manually keep the string pulled back while also aiming and shooting. Instead, the crossbow's body can hold the string, allowing the hunter to have a steadier aim. Crossbows are fast and accurate. The downsides are that they are slow to reload, noisy to shoot, and heavy to carry.

Some hunters find a crossbow easier to use than other bow types because they don't have to hold the string back while aiming.

Hunters using bows and arrows may want to bring some gear specifically for their equipment. A quiver is a container that holds arrows. The quiver may be worn on the hunter's back or hip. Some hunters choose to mount specially made quivers directly onto their bows. Another piece of gear when hunting

Quivers can be mounted onto compound bows.

A finger tab sits where the fingers pull the bowstring.

with a longbow or recurve bow is a finger tab. This small piece of leather protects the hunter's shooting finger from the bowstring. An arm guard is worn on the arm that is not used to draw the bow. An arm guard provides protection from the snap of the bowstring. A crossbow hunter may add a scope to the bow. This is a lens that the hunter looks through. It magnifies the target and helps the hunter aim.

TRAPS

When seeking fur-bearing game, hunters often use traps. The most common type is called a foothold trap. It is available in many sizes depending on what type of game is being trapped. Foothold traps work through the use of pressure. When an animal steps on the trap, two jaws on the trap close around the game's leg. The jaws of modern foothold traps are designed to be humane. Some have padded jaws or shock absorbers to prevent pain and injury to the animal. If an unintended animal is caught in the trap, the hunter can release it back into the wild without injury.

Modern foothold traps no longer have the jagged teeth they once did.

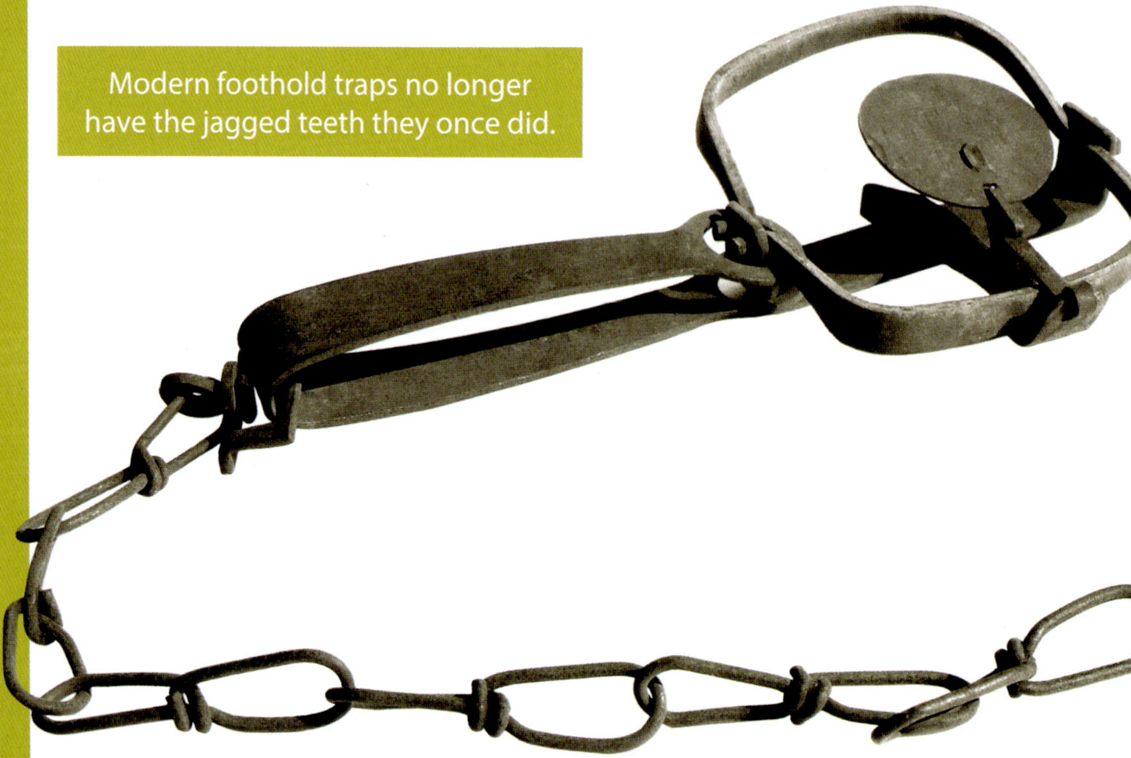

A hunter sets a Conibear trap to catch beavers.

Some hunters use body-grip traps, also known as Conibear traps after Frank Conibear, the man who invented them in the 1950s. These traps have two square frames that are connected to a spring. When triggered, these traps instantly kill the game. Beavers, minks, and muskrats are all commonly trapped this way.

Snares can be set to make them more likely to catch certain species, such as rabbits.

Another type of trap is called a snare. The snare is a wire loop that closes around an animal's foot when the animal steps in and pulls it. In the past, snares have accidentally trapped many nontarget animals. Today, a complex system of cables, locks, and swivels lets a snare be customized in many ways for the type of game and the location, reducing the problem. In addition, trappers can limit how small the loop can shrink and also add breakaway mechanisms so that powerful animals can pull free without injury.

No matter what type of trap is used, hunters must check their traps frequently. This will reduce the amount of time an animal is trapped. Any target game that is trapped must be killed quickly and humanely. Hunters must also take great care in placing their traps to avoid accidental trapping. For example, because of how deadly they are, Conibear traps should never be used in areas with pets who might walk into them accidentally.

Traps should be checked often so that animals in them do not suffer for long.

SITES, SCOUTING, AND TRACKING

Before heading out to the field, hunters must choose a site. One of the most important considerations is who owns the land. Many people choose to hunt on privately owned land. Hunters must get permission from landowners to do this. Each state has different laws, but in general, hunting on private land without permission is trespassing. In many states, trespassing can result in fines and the loss of a hunter's license.

Hunters should watch for signs that they are nearing private property.

Hunters may give landowners some of the meat from the game they shoot.

To get permission, hunters contact the landowner directly. They should introduce themselves and explain their interest in hunting on the land. Hunters might offer to do small jobs in exchange for using the land. This may include hauling wood or mending fences. Or they might share some of the game they harvest. Some landowners welcome hunters. Others will refuse. It's important to remain kind and polite no matter the response.

Hunters must hunt only in areas the landowner allows.

If permission is granted, hunters and landowners must maintain a clear line of communication. Landowners should tell hunters when and where they may hunt. Certain days, hours, or sections of the property may be off-limits to hunting. In turn, hunters should communicate when and where they plan to hunt. This communication ensures respect and safety during the hunting season.

Hunters are guests when on private land. They should never litter or leave behind any trace of their presence. They should never mark or cut trees, walk through crops without permission, start campfires, or move the position of any fence gates. Firearms should not be discharged near livestock or buildings. And hunters who bring hunting dogs with them need to keep the dogs under control while on private land. Hunters should inform landowners when they have completed their hunting. This will allow landowners to grant permission to other hunters who may wish to use the land as well.

Some landowners hunt too. If visiting hunters are around, landowners may organize their hunts for a different day.

PUBLIC LANDS

Public lands can also provide hunting opportunities. These lands are owned by the government. The federal government has public hunting lands in 400 wildlife refuges and 35 wetland districts. Each state also has its own public lands that grant access to hunters throughout the year. State lands total approximately 199 million acres (80.5 million ha).

People can hunt in certain state forests.

Hikers and other people using public land open to hunting should wear brightly colored clothing or backpacks to make them easy for hunters to see.

Depending on the year and the conditions, public lands may be more crowded with people than private lands. People enjoy hiking, fishing, canoeing, and other forms of outdoor recreation on public lands. To keep public land use a positive experience for everyone, hunters should always be respectful of others who are enjoying the land.

Private land will often have signs identifying it, but it is the responsibility of hunters to study maps ahead of time and plan their hunting zones.

Hunting is not permitted on all public land. Hunters must research whether the area they want to hunt in has been approved for hunting. This should include approval for the type of game they're seeking and the weapons they would like to use. They also need to know the boundaries of the public land. This can prevent a hunter from accidentally trespassing on private land. The best way to learn terrain is by studying maps.

DID YOU KNOW?

Alaska has the most public land of any state. Nearly 90 percent of the land is owned by the state or federal governments. A majority of that land is approved for hunting, and 15 percent of Alaskans have a hunting license.

Though public lands may be crowded, they have a wide variety of game. Depending on the location, game includes deer, wild hogs, turkeys, and many kinds of waterfowl. To find game, hunters often trek far from roads and established trails. This may mean fewer people, but it also has challenges. If a hunter downs large game, hauling it out of the field far from roads and trails can be difficult work. It may take two or more people to move an elk or deer. It is important to plan for this before taking a shot.

Hunters must be prepared to walk on uneven terrain.

SCOUTING

Once a hunter has chosen the land, the next step is scouting, or selecting a specific site. Some properties can be thousands of acres in size. Scouting can take time, effort, and planning. It is a good idea to do scouting work well ahead of the hunt. Hunters often start their scouting electronically. They rely on technology such as weather apps, online maps, and satellite images.

Hunting apps can allow hunters to view maps even if they have no cellular service in a hunting area.

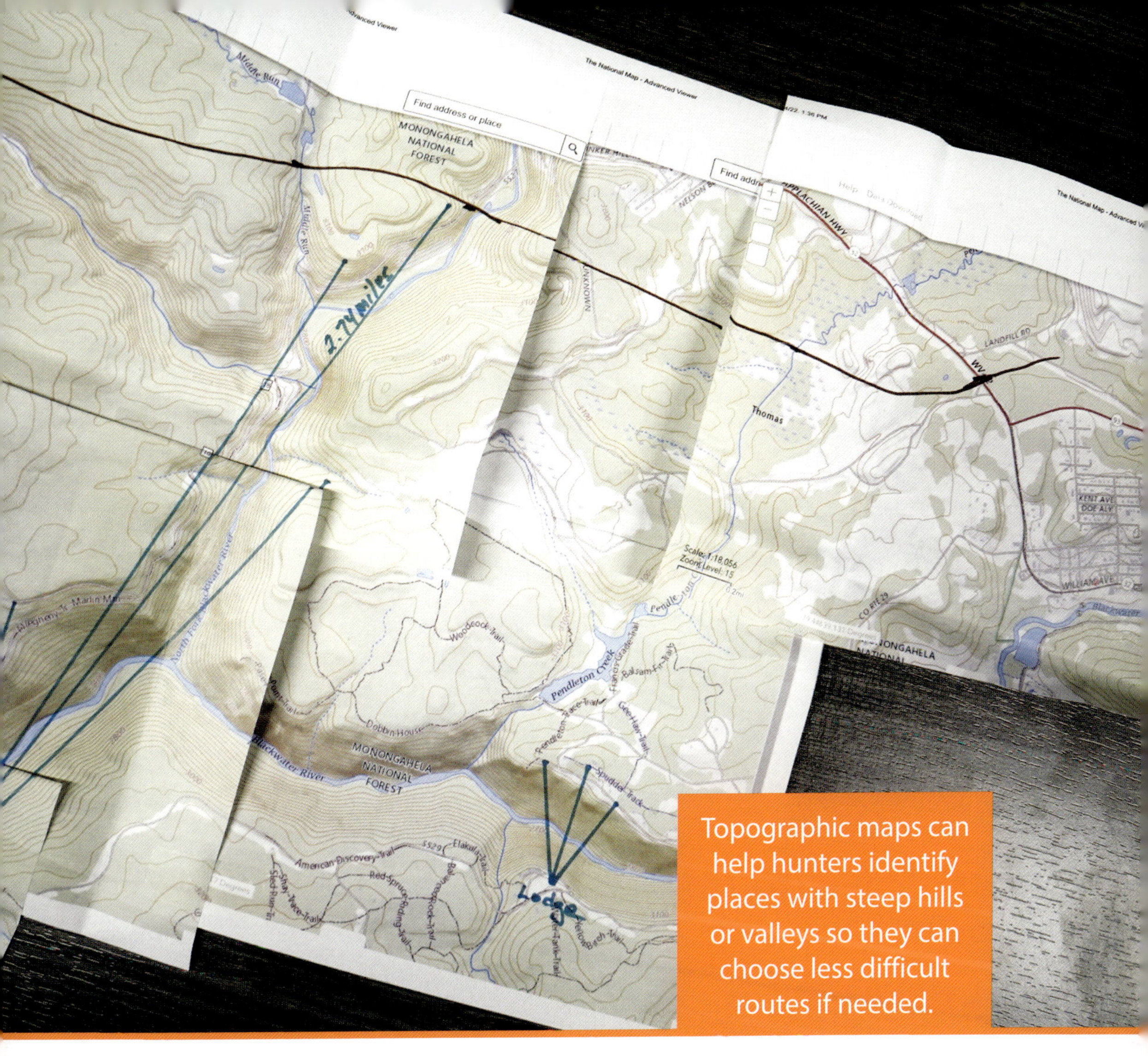

Topographic maps can help hunters identify places with steep hills or valleys so they can choose less difficult routes if needed.

Specialized hunting apps can provide much of the information needed to scout a site. These apps often feature a variety of maps tailored to the needs of hunters. Topographic maps show changes in terrain elevation. Aerial maps show property lines and what land is public or private. Hydrological maps show the locations of bodies of water. Maps made from satellite images can provide details about vegetation and tree cover.

White-tailed deer graze in fields near trees so they can easily see predators and escape to cover.

Based on the type of game a hunter is seeking, these maps can provide clues for good potential sites. Deer, for instance, are most likely to be found in transitional areas. This could be where the edge of a field meets a wooded area. Or the transitional area could be where two types of terrain meet, such as a drainage ditch along a piece of flat land. These areas can be identified using satellite mapping.

While the technology is helpful, it is no replacement for seeing the land in person. Some sites that look great on a map are disappointing in person. Sites that look questionable electronically may prove to have great potential. In-person scouting also provides a chance to see whether any signs of game are present at the site. All of these steps contribute to a successful hunt.

Hunters often give themselves time to select new sites if those originally selected show no signs of game.

TRACKING

Tracking is another way to find a good site. This is following signs animals leave behind. Animals leave signs of their movements wherever they go. Knowing how to identify these signs is a key skill for hunters. If hunters find many signs while tracking, they have likely found a site that holds promise for hunting.

The ability to track increases a hunter's chances of success.

White-tailed deer make many small, round droppings, *left*. Bears may have berries in their scat.

One of the easiest signs to observe is animal droppings. By examining the droppings, a hunter can tell what kind of animal has been in an area and how long ago. Herbivores, such as rabbits and deer, often produce small, round droppings. The droppings of carnivores and omnivores, such as wildcats or bears, are loose or long and tapered. Bird droppings may be liquid or solid, depending on their diets.

Snow can make it easier to find animal tracks.

Hunters also track animals by identifying their footprints, which are called tracks. The tracks animals leave can tell a hunter what direction an animal is headed. The spacing of the tracks can reveal how fast an animal was moving. The size of the tracks can also reveal the size of the animal. Tracks may lead to a den, nesting place, or feeding spot, which may be places for a hunter to set up.

RUBS AND SCRAPES

Some animal signs require an especially keen eye. Deer hunters, for example, often look for rubs and scrapes. Bucks rub their antlers on trees in the fall. This peels off the bark and leaves a bare spot called a rub. Finding many rubs in a close area means there's a good likelihood of finding a buck. Scrapes are formed on the ground under trees when deer paw at the ground. This is a way for deer to leave their scent. Like rubs, scrapes are a good sign that deer are in the area.

Each type of animal leaves a distinct footprint. Animals in the dog family, such as coyotes, have four toes on their front and back feet. Wild cats do as well. To tell the difference, a hunter must look to see if the tracks have claw marks. Cats withdraw their claws when they walk, while dogs do not. Tracks left by animals in the weasel family, such as badgers and minks, have five toes on their front and back feet. Bears have five toes too, though a bear's footprint would be much larger than that of a badger. Animals with hooves, such as deer and moose, can be identified by two toes.

Turkeys leave three-toed tracks. A smaller fourth toe, which points backward, does not always show in the tracks.

HUNTING STRATEGIES

Hunting strategies vary widely depending on the terrain, the weather, and the type of game. One thing they all have in common is the goal of concealing the hunter from the game. For visual concealment, hunters wear clothing that blends in with their surroundings. This breaks up the hunter's body shape, making him or her less visible. Hunters often dress in camouflage from head to toe, including a face mask or face paint. This is especially important

DID YOU KNOW?

A ghillie suit is a three-dimensional form of camouflage clothing. Pieces of fabric that mimic leaves, grasses, vines, and other types of vegetation are attached to the outside of the suit. This added texture breaks up a hunter's silhouette more than standard camouflage clothing.

Different patterns of camouflage work better against different types of scenery, such as branches or snow.

Hunters can choose to wear suits that look as if mosses and grasses are hanging off of them.

when hunting game that has good color vision, such as turkeys or waterfowl.

Another thing hunters must conceal is their scent. Most game animals have a keen sense of smell. If an animal smells a human, there is a good chance it will run off. To stop this from happening, hunters pay attention to the wind direction. It is best to be downwind of the game while in the field. This means the wind is at the hunter's face. Staying downwind blows a hunter's scent away from the game.

It's important for hunters to carefully choose each step to move as quietly as possible.

The final thing hunters must conceal is sound and movement. These often go together because moving quickly can be noisier than taking slow steps. Any sound, no matter how quiet, can alert the game to a hunter's presence. Clothing should not make any rustling sounds. Hunters must also be aware of what is on the ground in front of them before they take a step. The snap of a twig or the crunch of dry leaves can alert game to a hunter's presence. Moving quietly is often easier in wet conditions.

STALKING AND STILL HUNTING

Stalking is a hunting strategy of visually locating game from a distance. Then the hunter walks toward the game until it is within range. Stalking is typically used on large game, such as deer, elk, or caribou. Visually identifying game is often done from a site with a good vantage point, usually at a high elevation. Binoculars or scopes are especially useful tools for this task.

Hunters try to stay out of sight of the game when stalking.

Once game is spotted, hunters will examine the terrain to figure out the best path toward the animal. As the hunters begin to close the gap between themselves and the game, they try to remain as hidden as possible. They also stay out of the sight line of any game they are stalking. Brush, tall grasses, and trees provide the best cover. Hills, boulders, and other natural formations can also be used as cover for hunters.

When walking toward the game, hunters should remain downwind. As they close in on the target area, their movements must become increasingly slower. Each step should be chosen carefully to avoid any noise. As hunters near the game, they may need to pause frequently to watch. This will allow them to make any necessary adjustments so they can get into the best position for a shot.

The hunter can shoot when the game is in range and the hunter has a clear shot.

Because the goal of still hunting is to remain unseen by prey, it's especially important that still hunters wear blaze orange so other hunters can spot them.

Much like stalking, still hunting requires hunters to get physically close to the game they are seeking. Instead of following the game, however, still hunters wait for the game to come to them. They conceal themselves within a site that has a high likelihood of game passing through it. They remain still and silent, hiding in shadows, under brush, or behind trees. They observe everything in their surroundings and wait for the game to come close.

Still hunters spend about ten times longer waiting quietly than they do moving to a new waiting spot.

Still hunters do not remain stationary the entire time they are on the hunt. As they make tracking observations, hunters may choose to walk slowly within a small area to better position themselves. Much like stalking, still hunting requires a keen awareness of wind direction, sound, and movement. Still hunters generally stand and observe far more than they walk during a hunt.

HUNTING FROM A BLIND

Another common hunting strategy is referred to as ambush. Ambush-style hunters do not stalk their game. Instead, they remain hidden in one place, waiting for the game to come near. One of the most popular ways to do this is from a shelter called a blind. Blinds can be used to hunt many types of game, from ducks and turkeys to deer and elk. Hunters wait inside the blind, sometimes for many hours. They scan the terrain from the blind's openings. When game comes within range, they shoot.

Hunting blinds can be tent-like shelters with camouflage patterns.

Hunting from a blind has many advantages. Blinds hide hunters in shadow, allowing them to move undetected. This creates more time to set up a shot. A blind also helps conceal the hunter's scent from the game and provides protection from the sun, wind, and rain. The disadvantage is that blinds can be cramped inside. And shooting options are limited to the openings in the blind.

Some blinds are built into the ground.

Hunters watch for game through openings in the blind.

Blinds come in a variety of styles. Some are made to sit directly on the ground. These are called ground blinds, and they can be temporary or permanent. At their most rugged, ground blinds can be built using vegetation or tarps that are camouflaged with brush. Pop-up ground blinds can be purchased at sporting goods stores. They look much like a camouflaged tent. They can easily be set up on any site the hunter believes is promising.

Gun clubs or landowners may put up permanent ground stands on hunting lands.

Some hunters prefer to use permanent ground stands. These stands remain in the same site and are usually made of wood and metal. The benefit is that the hunter doesn't have to spend time setting up each time he or she hunts. Because this type of blind is made of sturdier materials, it is usually warmer than a pop-up blind. The disadvantage is that this kind of blind cannot be moved. A hunter is stuck at the site even if the game is not nearby.

Permanent blinds can be placed on the ground or elevated. Elevated blinds are on a stand that is several feet off the ground. A ladder on the outside of the blind allows the hunter to get inside. Elevated stands give hunters a better viewpoint of the game. Most also offer 360-degree views. Also, missed shots taken from an elevated stand will generally hit the ground rather than potentially hitting an unintended target.

Elevated blinds can make it even harder for game to spot the hunter.

HUNTING FROM A TREE STAND

Much like an elevated blind, tree stands raise hunters off the ground. They are another way to practice the ambush-style hunting strategy. Tree stands are platforms with ladders that hunters can bring to the field and place in a tree of their choosing. They are typically set up in a tree between 8 and 16 feet (2.4 and 4.9 m) off the ground. Because they are portable, hunters can move them to a new tree if conditions change.

Many hunters like hang-on tree stands. They have a small platform for standing and a seat above it to sit on. The entire structure is secured to the tree using belts or chains. Hang-on tree stands are lightweight. They do not come with ladders, so hunters must use either screw-in steps or climbing sticks to set them up.

Because tree stands can be moved, they offer more choices in hunting spots than permanent blinds.

An experienced hunter can set up a hang-on tree stand in approximately 20 minutes.

SCREW-IN STEPS AND CLIMBING STICKS

Not all tree stands come with ladders. Some require either screw-in steps or walking sticks. Screw-in steps are thick metal rods shaped like the letter *L*. At one end they have a screw that can be driven into the tree trunk. Several of these placed up the length of a tree trunk serve as a makeshift ladder. Climbing sticks look like the steps of a ladder connected to a rod. The rods can be joined together and then fastened to the tree with belts to make a tall ladder.

Hunters should consider how easily moveable they would like their tree stand to be before purchasing one.

Like hang-on stands, climbing stands have a seat and platform. To install this style of stand, hunters attach the sections to the base of the tree using straps that grip the trunk. They place their weight on the top section, lifting the bottom section up with their feet. They then stand on the bottom section and push up the seat. They repeat this process, climbing up the tree with both sections of the stand.

Ladder tree stands are larger and heavier than the other two types. They take multiple people to install. Most hunters choose to do this the day before the hunt. This style of stand has a ladder attached to the platform and bench. The ladder with the seat and platform at the top is leaned against the tree trunk and secured using belts or chains. The ladder stand is the easiest to climb in and out of.

Ladder tree stands are the least portable of the tree stands.

No matter which style of tree stand a hunter uses, a safety harness is a must. This can keep a hunter from falling out of the tree stand.

HUNTING FROM A BOAT

Not all hunters stay on land. Those who are in search of waterfowl often hunt from boats. They must follow all hunting laws and all boating laws. Hunting boats are generally small and have flat bottoms. These features allow hunters to navigate shallow water. When the water is calm, the flat-bottomed boats stay in place and are relatively stable.

Hunting boats may be painted in a camouflage pattern.

Hunting boats should be stable.

Hunters must take extra precautions when in a boat. The boat should never be overloaded with people or gear. This could lead to the boat tipping over or dipping below the water's surface and filling with water. Firearms should be unloaded with the safety on while the boat is in motion to prevent any accidents. All hunters should remain seated and wear life jackets.

HUNTING WITH DOGS

Hunting dogs help hunters find game more quickly.

Dogs have been helping humans hunt for thousands of years. Hunting and tracking are natural instincts for many dog breeds. In the field, the hunter and dog work as partners. Dogs can help hunters locate game as well as ensure that any game that has been shot is quickly found and retrieved.

DID YOU KNOW?

In 2017, archaeologists in Saudi Arabia found stone carvings that showed dogs helping humans hunt gazelles and ibex. The carvings are from between 8,000 and 9,000 years ago.

Getting a dog ready for the hunt takes training and practice. Well-trained hunting dogs are not startled by the sound of a firearm discharging. When birds are flushed, or chased from hiding, the dog should remain still until the hunter releases it with a command. This is for the dog's safety so that it is not accidentally shot.

It takes a lot of training to prevent hunting dogs from becoming afraid of gunshots.

Hunters have many breeds to choose from when looking for a hunting companion. Usually, hunters will choose a dog that is a good match for the kind of game they are hunting. Hunters will look for dogs that can do well in their preferred hunting terrains, whether that is near water, in tall grasslands, or in heavily forested land. They also pay attention to any special skills the dogs may be bred to have that will help in the field. These skills include pointing, flushing, retrieving, and hounding.

Certain breeds, such as golden retrievers, are better suited than some other hunting breeds for tasks involving cold water.

Sometimes a pointer will lift one paw or hold its tail straight out from its body when on point.

POINTERS AND FLUSHERS

Pointers and flushers are dogs that are bred to find birds. For this reason, both are considered bird dogs. Their main uses in the field are to help hunters find, flush, and retrieve upland game birds.

Pointers are athletic dogs that can run long distances when on the scent of game birds. When they close in on the game, pointers freeze. They stand still, with their bodies pointed in the direction of the game. They remain still until the hunter gives them the command to release.

Related to the German shorthaired pointer, the German wirehaired pointer is another common pointing breed.

While the pointer remains still, the hunter decides how best to set up a shot. Then the hunter gives a command, the pointer flushes the birds, and the hunter shoots. Pointers are most useful in hunting birds that don't immediately fly when danger is first detected. This includes game birds such as grouse, pheasants, or quails. Breeds that make good pointers include German shorthaired pointers, Irish setters, and Brittanys.

Flushers have similar skills to pointers, though they approach the hunt a bit differently. Pointers freeze when they find game, but flushers do the opposite. Flushers chase the game birds out of their hiding places and into flight without pausing. Pointers run long distances from hunters in search of game. Flushers stay much closer to the hunters, usually within shotgun range.

Flushing dogs cause game birds to take flight so the hunter can shoot.

When a dog is getting ready to flush, its tail will wag faster, and its movements will focus on one area. This behavior is a signal to the hunter to get ready to shoot. In addition to game birds, flushers can also flush small game such as rabbits. These dogs are skilled at working in a variety of settings, including grasslands, woodlands, and swamps. Breeds that make good flushers are the English springer spaniel, the American water spaniel, and the Boykin spaniel.

Many hunting breeds, including the English springer spaniel, have lines that are bred mainly for hunting.

Retrievers can be especially useful for retrieving game from water.

RETRIEVERS

Retrievers are used in the collection of waterfowl that has been shot down. During the hunt, retrievers stay quietly at the side of the hunter. After the hunter shoots the game, the retriever steps in. The dog picks up and returns the downed bird to the hunter. This can involve swimming in lakes, rivers, and swamps, or traversing through fields, woodlands, and grasslands.

Retrievers have been bred for centuries with special traits that make them especially good at their job.

Retrievers have soft mouths. This means they can pick up, hold, and carry game birds gently. Many retrieving breeds have fur that is water repellant, which helps them stay dry and warm when doing water retrievals. Common breeds include the golden retriever and the Labrador retriever. Pointers and flushers can often be trained to retrieve too.

EARTHDOGS

Terriers are a type of earthdog. They are bred to hunt small burrowing animals, such as mice and rats. These types of dogs are useful at keeping farms free from pests. Some terriers can also be used to hunt game such as rabbits, squirrels, badgers, and foxes.

HOUNDS

Hounds are dogs that pursue game and bring a hunter to it. This type of hunting is called hounding. Hound dogs fall into two categories: scent hounds and sight hounds. Scent hounds use mainly their keen sense of smell to track game. Sight hounds use mainly their sharp vision to find and chase after game. Hounds cover large distances and can help hunters pursue a great variety of game. They can track small game, such as raccoons, rabbits, and squirrels. They are also good at pursuing large game including foxes, coyotes, deer, wild hogs, bears, and wild cats.

Elkhounds help hunters track wounded game.

Before the hunt, the hound is fitted with a Global Positioning System (GPS) collar. This allows hunters to keep track of the hound's exact location. To begin a hunt, the hunters release the hounds. Hounds often work in packs. When they find a scent, the dogs work together to track it. Ideally, the hounds corner the game. For example, they may chase a bear into a tree or surround a wild hog on all sides. They tell the hunter that they have cornered the game by baying.

When this happens, the hunters use the GPS collars and the sound of the baying to find the hounds. When hunters arrive at the site, they have two choices. They may call off the hounds and release the game. Or they may shoot the game.

Some hounds hold large game in one area until the hunter arrives to shoot it.

Coonhounds run racoons up trees and let out loud barks so the hunters can find them.

Common scent hound breeds for hunting include the American coonhound, the beagle, and the Plott hound. Fewer people hunt with sight hounds in the United States, but the greyhound is sometimes used to hunt coyotes. Laws around hunting with hounds vary. States where it is legal may have restrictions on what type of game may be pursed. Hunters who want to go out with their hounds must follow all state and local laws.

A leash can help hunting dogs learn when to stay close to their handlers.

TRAINING

Before a dog is ready to head out with a hunter, it needs to be properly trained. Without good training, a dog may scare off prey rather than aid a hunter. Training requires patience and care. Training is not just about learning commands. It is also a bonding time between the dog and the hunter. It gives them a chance to learn how to work with each other. This understanding will make being out in the field more enjoyable for both of them.

One of the most basic elements of training a hunting dog is obedience. Dogs used for hunting should learn basic commands such as sit, stay, and come. Later, more complex commands can be added. This might include teaching a dog to retrieve. For puppies, this might look like a simple game of fetch. Fetching can start out with toys or a pheasant wing. As the dog improves and gets older, it can then move to dummies that look, feel, and smell like whole game.

Training a hunting dog often begins while puppies are still with their breeders.

Another part of training is making sure the dog gets used to the sound of gunshots. This loud noise can startle some dogs. The exposure to loud noises should begin gradually. A hunter may make loud, sharp noises around the house. This could involve clanging pots together, loudly closing cabinet doors, or sounding an alarm on a phone. Trying to connect the loud sound with something rewarding, such as going outside to play, will help.

Owners can make loud noises while their dogs eat to help them associate noises with good things.

Some people train their own dogs for hunting, and others send their dogs to professional trainers.

Eventually, the dog will be ready to hear the discharge of a firearm. This should also be done gradually and with a lot of support. One way to do this is with a hunting friend. The owner can play with the dog while the friend discharges the weapon far away. Gradually the sounds can become closer and louder, as long as the dog remains comfortable. When the training is done, the hunter should be able to discharge the firearm near the dog without the dog flinching.

AFTER THE HUNT

Scent hounds such as beagles make great tracking dogs, but many other dogs can be trained for this job as well.

When hunters make a solid shot, the next phase of the hunt begins. Hunters must find the game that they have taken down. When hunting birds with a dog, the job of retrieving the downed animals belongs to the dog. But when hunting large game, this job usually falls to the hunter. It is the ethical responsibility of the hunter to track the wounded game until all reasonable efforts to find it have been exhausted.

Tracking wounded game is not always an easy task. When an animal is shot, it often runs off in a panic. At the time of the shot, the hunter should take note of what direction the animal fled. When the animal is out of sight, listening for its sounds can also provide clues. Unless the hunter can see the downed animal, he or she should wait between 15 and 30 minutes before beginning to track it. Tracking it right away will cause the game to feel pursued. Its adrenaline will make it travel farther, and it will be more difficult to find.

Wounded game can travel long distances.

At that point, the hunter must look for clues left by the game as it ran off. This could include tracks, blood, or hair. Many hunters mark the trail as they go, using a biodegradable product such as toilet paper that won't harm the environment if the hunters can't find every piece when they're done. A flashlight can help when the tracking happens after dark.

It helps to know the tracks of the species being hunted in order to follow wounded game.

Tracking takes focus and practice.

When the downed animal has been spotted, the hunter must approach it with caution. If its eyes are open, the hunter should poke it with a stick near the eye. If the animal does not blink, it is probably no longer alive. If the animal is wounded but still breathing, the hunter must fire a final shot to end its life.

Hunters need to fill out information on a game tag, such as when and where the animal was shot.

Once an animal has been harvested, the hunter has two responsibilities. The first is to record and tag the kill as required by local laws. The second is to move the carcass. Some large game, such as elk or moose, can be quite heavy and may require at least two hunters to move. Traditionally, game was used as a source of food. Today, many hunters continue the tradition of eating the game they hunt. To do so requires special skills in the field to be undertaken quickly. This will prevent the game from rotting and going to waste.

FIELD DRESSING

Field dressing is the process of removing an animal's entrails, which are its internal organs. The faster this step can be completed the better. Removing the entrails cools the body of the game quickly. It slows the growth of bacteria in the game, which is important for preventing foodborne illnesses. It also improves the flavor of the meat. The basic tools for field dressing are a sharp knife, latex gloves, alcohol swabs, and paper towels. Depending on conditions, bags of ice, rope, and game bags may be necessary as well.

Big game such as deer are heavy and difficult to move.

To start, the hunter should put on latex gloves. The gloves protect him or her from any disease the game might be carrying. Next, the hunter makes a cut from the breastbone downward. This can be done with the game lying on its back or hung from a tree. The most important thing to remember when making cuts is to prevent the spread of bacteria. To do this, hunters should clean their knives frequently using alcohol swabs. Hunters should also use great care not to nick the intestines, as this can release bacteria.

With the cut made, the hunter then uses a gloved hand to remove the entrails. Once the body cavity has been emptied, hunters should wipe away any remaining blood

Some hunters wear shoulder-length gloves when cleaning big game.

A sharp knife will help the cleaning process go quickly.

inside with paper towels. The emptied carcass should never be stored in direct sunlight. Heat can make bacteria grow in it more quickly. If the air temperature is above 40 degrees Fahrenheit (4.4°C), the cavity should be packed with ice-filled bags. If the temperature is below 40 degrees Fahrenheit (4.4°C), the carcass is safe to leave outside for a longer period.

CHRONIC WASTING DISEASE

Chronic wasting disease (CWD) affects game such as deer, elk, and moose. The disease causes animals to lose weight, stumble, and become listless. According to the Centers for Disease Control and Prevention, CWD is not known to be transmitted to people through infected animals. However, hunters should still take all the precautions when field dressing game. Meat can be tested for CWD. Any meat that tests positive should not be eaten.

Skinning removes both the skin and fur from the animal.

SKINNING AND TRANSPORTING

After the entrails are removed, the hunter must decide what to do with the hide. Some hunters chose to skin their game while still in the field. Skinning is the process of removing the hide from the carcass. The hide acts as a kind of insulation. Skinning the hide can speed up the cooling process of the carcass, which is helpful on a hot day. It can also keep the hide in good condition if the hunter plans to bring it to a taxidermist.

Skinning game requires practice and patience. The person doing the skinning must be careful not to let the knife accidentally puncture the meat. Every time this happens, the meat has a new entry point for bacteria. And when skinning the hide, the hunter must take care not to cut the hide itself. This can lead to hair or fur from the hide falling onto the meat. Skinned animals should be placed in food-grade game bags to keep them free of insects, dirt, leaves, and other debris.

Some hunters send skins to a taxidermist to make mountings to display in their homes.

Not all hunters choose to skin their game in the field. If the temperature is cool enough, hunters may keep the hide on the game. It also makes hauling the game from the field to a campsite or a vehicle a bit easier. The hide can keep the carcass relatively clean and damage free when the hunter transports it out of the field.

Hunters may wait until they get home to skin their game.

Hunters pluck feathers by hand.

Fowl is treated much the same way as large game. Some hunters choose to skin their fowl in the field, especially if the meat will later be cubed or ground. Some hunters plan to roast or deep-fry the fowl whole. In this case, they generally do not skin the bird. Instead, they pluck the feathers from it. To make plucking the feathers easier, some hunters scald the fowl first. This involves dipping the fowl into boiling water, which loosens the feathers.

When hunting large game, hunters need a vehicle big enough to haul the animal.

Whether skinned or not, at this point, the carcass is ready to transport. As with all the steps in field dressing, this one requires an attention to food safety guidelines. Hunters often transport their game in the beds of pickup trucks or on trailers. Whichever is chosen should be lined with a tarp, as well as covered with one. This will prevent dirt, rain, snow, or road grime from getting onto the carcass. If temperatures are warm, bags of ice should be packed around the carcass to slow the growth of bacteria.

BUTCHERING

Some hunters take their game to a facility that butchers the carcass for them. Professional butchers have specialized tools and are skilled at this work. They may also offer services to cure or smoke the meat, as well as make it into sausages.

Butchers typically require that animals have tags to ensure the animals were harvested legally.

Some hunters prefer to do the butchering themselves. It can be completed in the field immediately after removing the entrails. Or it can be done once the game has been transported to another location, such as a hunter's garage. Sporting goods stores sell butchering kits. They typically contain a variety of knives, a knife sharpener, a bone saw, a rib-cage spreader, a cutting board, and gloves. Having the proper tools, especially sharp knives, makes the butchering much easier.

Bone saws, *right*, have jagged blades.

Hunters butchering their own meat may also grind some of the meat to be used for burgers or other dishes.

When in the field, it is easiest to hang large game from a tree for the butchering. Many hunters use the rafters in their garages in the same way when butchering deer at home. Hunters may follow the basic meat-cutting charts for large game that butchers use for domestic animals such as hogs and cattle. Hunters may butcher the meat into steaks, chops, or cubes for stew. They may also grind some of the meat to make sausages or burgers.

Hunters who use lead shot or bullets should carefully check their meat for lead.

Hunters who butcher their own game must pay attention to one extra food-safety issue. Meat near the entry point of a bullet may not be safe to eat. This potential safety issue applies to game that has been taken down using lead shot or a lead bullet. Lead is not safe to consume. Pieces of the ammunition can fracture upon impact and become lodged in the meat. Any damaged meat surrounding an entry point should be trimmed away and thrown out. This prevents any stray lead from the ammunition from being consumed.

EATING THE GAME

Some game, such as deer or elk, can provide a large quantity of meat. Most hunters cannot eat it all before it spoils. Many decide to freeze the meat to use it later. The meat can be packed in freezer paper, aluminum foil, or food-storage bags. Hunters should be sure any extra fat has been trimmed off the meat before freezing it. Fat from game animals can turn rancid in the freezer and spoil the meat. This is especially true of venison, or deer meat.

Hunters may have freezers for storing a lot of meat.

Not all hunters want to keep the meat from all the game they hunt. Many states offer programs that allow hunters to donate meat to food shelves. These programs provide a source of high-quality protein to people who are food insecure. It's not as simple as dropping off a few steaks at the food shelf, however. Hunters who participate in donation programs must follow special guidelines to ensure food safety.

DID YOU KNOW?

Game donations make a big difference to people in need. In South Dakota, hunters donated 18,615 pounds (8,444 kg) of game meat in the 2021–2022 hunting season. Since the state's program began in 1993, it has provided more than 1 million pounds (453,000 kg) of game meat to residents.

Hunters may donate entire animals in some places.

Some local meat processors will butcher game donated to food shelves.

Safety guidelines for donated meat vary by state. In Wisconsin, for example, hunters who want to donate meat must agree to specific field dressing methods. Only carcasses are accepted, not meat that has already been butchered. Any donated game carcasses must have their hides intact. A hunter brings the carcass to be butchered at a meat processing plant that is approved by the state's department of agriculture. These guidelines are to prevent foodborne illnesses.

ETHICS, CONSERVATION, AND LAWS

Hunting laws exist for many reasons, including to protect species populations.

Ethics, conservation, and laws form the bedrock of legal hunting in the United States today. Ethics are the code of behavior that a hunter follows while out in the field. Conservation is the practice of protecting and preserving wildlife for future generations. Laws set boundaries on what game is legal to hunt and when, as well as how much game a hunter can harvest from the wild.

Hunting ethics center on respect for wildlife. One of the ways hunters demonstrate this is with the fair chase. The fair chase is a way to keep the hunter and the game evenly matched. Its goal is to prevent a hunter from having an unfair advantage. An example of an unfair advantage might be shooting game from moving car or boat. Another example might be hunting game that is enclosed by a fence. These are considered unethical practices by many hunters.

Besides giving a hunter an unfair advantage, shooting from a moving boat can also be dangerous to people around the hunter.

In some cases, the ethics of a hunt are not set in stone. They can vary greatly from region to region. For example, hunting with hounds is legal and considered ethical by many people in the southern United States. This same practice in northeastern states is illegal and often considered unethical. Even if a

Hunters may wait until a bird is in flight before shooting so the bird has more of a chance to escape.

It can be easy to get impatient, but waiting for a clean shot is important.

hunting method is legal, some hunters may find it unethical. For example, it might be legal to shoot ducks that are on the water. Yet a hunter might personally believe the practice is unethical and decide not to do it.

Another ethical ideal that hunters follow is making a quick, clean kill. Hunters should fire only when they have a good shot. This means having a clear view of the target and being within the range of the firearm or bow. A well-placed shot can kill an animal quickly. This cuts down on pain and suffering for the animal.

The gray wolf was overhunted in the United States. Conservation efforts have helped the population grow again.

A poor shot happens when the hunter doesn't have a good view or the bullet hits the edge of a branch or other obstacle, causing it to shift direction. This may wound the game, making it suffer. Wounded animals are also difficult to track and recover.

CONSERVATION

Federal and state laws govern hunting in the United States. These laws protect wild game while at the same time permitting people to hunt legally. They also keep hunters and nonhunters alike safe while outdoors during hunting seasons. Many laws are driven by conservation efforts. They ensure that the game populations are closely monitored to remain stable. This will ensure that the sport of hunting remains strong for future generations.

Early in the nation's history, there were no hunting regulations. Game such as wild turkeys, bison, deer, elk, and mountain goats were abundant. People could hunt whatever game they found in the wild. They did not have limits on how many of each animal they killed.

White settlers hunted the bison to near extinction by the late 1800s.

Theodore Roosevelt served as US president and lived from 1858 to 1919.

The Boone and Crockett Club has published many books about hunting.

The hunting free-for-all eventually created problems. It led to the overhunting of some types of game, such as wild turkeys and bison, which nearly went extinct. Some species, including the passenger pigeon, were hunted to extinction. Hunters began to think about how to conserve the nation's wildlife.

Two leaders in the conservation movement were Theodore Roosevelt and George Bird Grinnell. In 1887, they formed the Boone and Crockett Club. It is the nation's oldest wildlife conservation group. The Boone and Crockett Club tries to balance the needs of hunters with the needs of wildlife. Its members introduced the nation's earliest conservation laws.

The Federal Aid in Wildlife Restoration Program supports state wildlife agencies.

Many of these early hunting and conservation laws are still in place today, such as the Wildlife Restoration Act of 1937. This federal law gives money to the states to conserve wildlife and their habitats. The act has helped restore game species that were once in danger of extinction, such as the wild turkey and the white-tailed deer.

Many conservationists view hunters as their partners. When they work together, they can keep game populations healthy. Conservationists may notice a deer population in a specific area is growing too large, for example. This can make it difficult for the animals to find food or shelter, leading to starvation and suffering. If too many deer are living near roads, dangerous car-deer accidents can become common. Hunting can help by keeping the deer population balanced. It stops overpopulation while laws prevent extinction.

Ducks Unlimited is an organization that supports the restoration and conservation of wetland habitats. Ninety percent of its members are hunters.

The joint efforts between conservationists and hunters have paid off. Early conservation efforts grew slowly and steadily over time. Today, the United States has the world's most successful wildlife conservation system.

LAWS

State laws conserve wildlife for the future. Laws vary in each state, but they are easy to find. Each state publishes its hunting regulations and laws in a handbook. These are available online through the state's wildlife conservation department. Local sporting stores often have printed copies of the handbook. Hunters are responsible for knowing the laws and regulations of the state where they are hunting. State conservation officers ensure that hunting laws are being followed.

NORTH AMERICAN WILDLIFE CONSERVATION MODEL

The United States and Canada have the world's leading system of wildlife conservation. This system has several goals, including conserving wildlife for the future. It ensures all citizens can hunt and all hunting laws will be made by citizens and their government. No wildlife can be hunted commercially or killed without a specific purpose. It views wildlife as an international resource to be managed by the best science available.

Public land may have park signs with postings about some regulations.

Laws determine each state's hunting seasons. A hunting season is the period of days, weeks, or months when hunting is legal for a specific type of game. Hunting seasons are carefully timed. They do not occur when animals are mating. Hunting during this time could be harmful to the future population. Instead, a hunting season typically aligns with the time when an animal's population is at its yearly high. Deer hunting, for example, is typically in the fall. Hunting game out of season is called poaching. It is illegal.

Geese are among the many animals that have young in the spring, so they cannot be hunted at this time.

Some areas of the country do not allow people to hunt does at all.

During each hunting season, state laws limit how much wildlife a hunter can harvest. This is often called a bag limit. Other limits also exist. Some states may outlaw targeting fawns during deer hunting season. Allowing the fawns to grow into adults keeps the overall deer population strong. Similarly, doe tags are also often limited. This ensures that enough does remain in a herd to reproduce the next year.

Bait is used to attract animals such as hogs or deer.

In a hunting season, laws determine what type of equipment and methods a hunter may use. Some seasons are reserved for bowhunting, while other dates are set aside for hunting with firearms. Laws may prohibit certain types of hunting methods as well. For example, in some states, baiting is illegal for certain types of game. Baiting involves setting out food that will attract a specific animal. This alters an animal's natural movements in the wild. It can concentrate an animal population on small parcels of land that have lots of bait.

DID YOU KNOW?

Money for the Wildlife Restoration Act comes from taxes on the manufacturing of hunting goods. These include firearms, ammunition, and supplies for bows and arrows. Since the act began in 1937, it has provided more than $22 billion for conservation projects and hunting education.

State laws determine other aspects of hunting that are not related strictly to conservation. They set a minimum age to hunt legally and determine what kind of hunting license a person needs. Safety and training requirements for hunters are determined by law. Laws also determine what kinds of permits, licenses, and background checks are required to obtain a firearm. Following all these laws makes hunting a safe and enjoyable sport.

Wildlife officials can check hunters' licenses.

SAFETY

Hunting has the potential to be a dangerous sport. Firearms, unpredictable weather, and wild animals all bring their own challenges. Before heading out to the field, hunters must be prepared to meet these challenges in a safe and responsible way. The most basic safety practice is to communicate. Hunters should tell someone where they will be, who is coming with them, and when they will return. This information can be lifesaving if a hunter needs emergency help.

Beginning hunters can go with experienced hunters to learn more about hunting safety.

Trained instructors teach firearm safety courses.

SAFETY COURSES

All states offer hunting safety courses. Many of these courses are overseen by the International Hunter Education Association-USA (IHEA-USA). Each year, IHEA-USA courses train 600,000 students to safely hunt and handle firearms. Since the program started in 1949, it has trained nearly 40 million students. In that time, the number of hunting accidents and injuries has dropped dramatically.

Students often get practice shooting guns as part of firearm safety courses.

All states except Alaska require a hunter to complete safety courses before he or she can get a hunting license. Alaska does require a safety course before hunting in certain areas and for people born in 1986 or later. The types of courses offered vary by state, so hunters should research the specific requirements in the area where they plan to hunt. This information is available on each state's natural resources web page. Some courses can be completed online, while others require being in a classroom or in the field. Prices for the courses vary. Some are free, while others have a fee.

Topics covered in hunting safety courses are wide-ranging. They may include the safe operations of firearms, bows, and traps. Other topics covered include conservation, ethics, game identification, survival skills, and first aid. States offer courses specifically geared toward young people as well as adults.

An instructor shows how to keep a finger off the trigger while holding a gun.

FIREARM SAFETY

Knowing how to handle a firearm safely is one of the most important parts of hunting. Firearm safety has four basic rules, which can prevent accidents, injuries, and deaths.

First, hunters should always assume their firearms are loaded. Even if a hunter knows a firearm is unloaded, he or she should treat it as if it were. Accidents have happened when a hunter thought a gun was unloaded and then pulled the trigger. Assuming a firearm is always loaded is acknowledging the responsibility of handling a firearm. It is also a sign of respect for any people nearby who could be put in danger by an unwanted discharge.

Always treating a firearm as if it were loaded helps prevent deadly accidents.

When out with other people, hunters should always be aware of where the other people are and never point a firearm in their direction.

Second, hunters should always be aware of where a firearm's muzzle is pointed. Anywhere the muzzle is pointed is a potential target. Approximately one-third of hunting injuries are self-inflicted. This means the hunter had the muzzle of the firearm pointed at some part of his or her own body when it discharged. These accidents can be prevented by making sure that the muzzle is not pointed toward anyone.

Hunters need to always be aware of their surroundings before shooting.

Third, hunters should be certain of the target before shooting. Taking a shot without being certain is reckless and could endanger other hunters who are in the field. Even if hunters are certain of the target, they may miss the shot. This may result in the bullet hitting an unintended target. For this reason, hunters must be aware of what is in in front of and behind the target before shooting.

Fourth, a hunter's finger should remain off the trigger until he or she is ready to take a shot. This is to prevent an unwanted discharge. For instance, if a hunter is walking and trips while a finger is on the trigger, the fall could discharge the firearm at an unintended target.

EXTRA PROTECTION

Firearms are often discharged while resting against the hunter's shoulder and cheek. His or her ears and eyes need to be protected. Firearms are loud when they are discharged, so many hunters wear ear protection to save their hearing. A discharge can also result in gases and particles in the air. To protect their eyes, many hunters wear safety glasses.

A hunter should keep his or her finger off the trigger even when lining up for the shot.

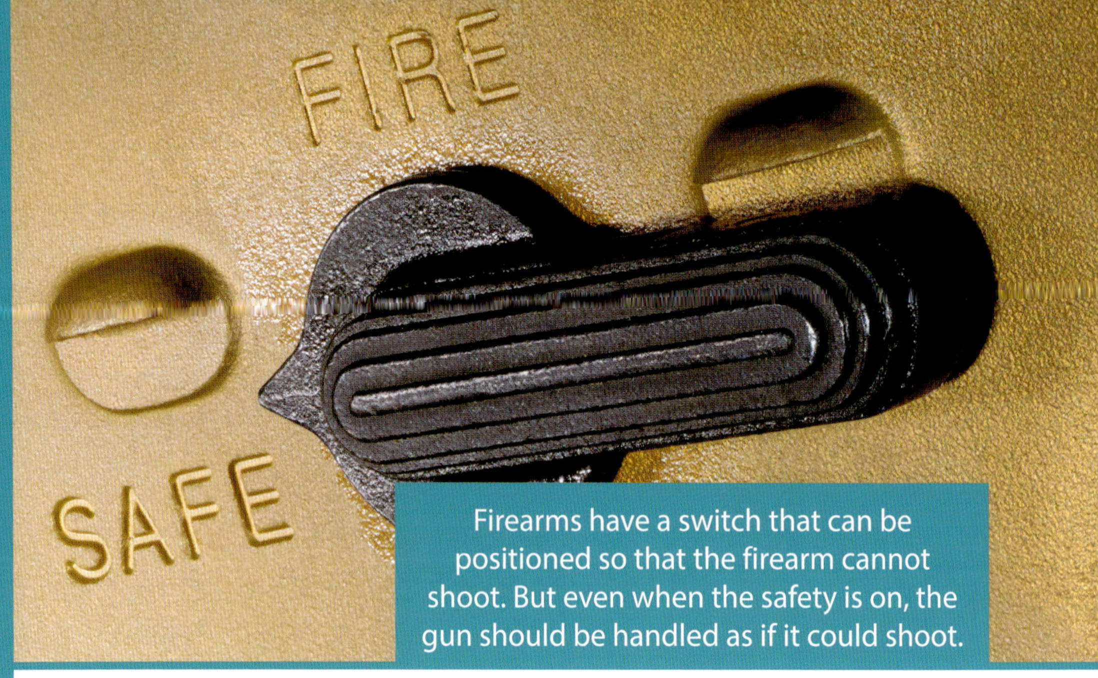

Firearms have a switch that can be positioned so that the firearm cannot shoot. But even when the safety is on, the gun should be handled as if it could shoot.

Even when a firearm is not being actively used, it still must be handled and cared for properly. The safety should always be engaged when the firearm is not in use. Hunters should also clean and maintain their firearms regularly. This will keep the firearm working as expected. When not in use, firearms should be unloaded. Ammunition and firearms should be stored separately and securely out of the reach of children.

TREE STAND SAFETY

Many people enjoy hunting from tree stands. But tree stands also come with risks. Every year across the nation, between 3,000 and 4,000 hunters are injured when they fall from tree stands. Following basic safety guidelines can reduce the chance of a fall.

Using a harness and a well-secured climbing rope increases a hunter's safety in a tree stand. If the hunter loses his or her balance, the harness and rope will stop the fall before the person reaches the ground. Full-body harnesses have straps that go over the shoulders, around each leg, and around the waist. It is nearly impossible for a hunter to fall out of this type of harness. Harnesses should be easy to use and worn every time a hunter goes into a tree stand.

Harnesses keep hunters from serious injury if they fall from a deer stand.

The tree a hunter selects also plays a role in tree stand safety. A mature tree with a sturdy, straight trunk and rough bark is generally safe. Trees with smooth bark can become slippery when wet with dew or rain. This makes them more difficult to climb and can also cause tree stands to shift in high winds. Living trees are also safer than dead trees. Wood on dead trees may be rotten and crumbling in places, which could lead to falls.

WEATHER SAFETY

Weather is another major safety issue. It affects all hunters, no matter what type of game they are hunting. Staying safe outside in rapidly changing conditions requires preparation. Many hunting seasons are in the fall, when weather can change quickly. A brisk, sunny afternoon can easily give way to a cold evening with rain or flurries. Being prepared for all these potential conditions is essential. Hunters should always check local forecasts before heading out.

Hunters should be prepared for the weather before they head out.

Once in the field, keeping an eye out for storms is important. Some hunters do this by bringing a portable weather radio. Improved cellular service in remote areas has allowed a growing number of hunters to rely on their mobile phones for weather updates. With either device, it is important not to waste the batteries. Being stuck outside with an incoming storm and no way to monitor the weather is dangerous.

Lightning is dangerous. Hunters should find shelter if a storm approaches.

In cold or wet weather, a hunter's gear becomes critical. Wet clothing can lower a person's body temperature. Hunters should avoid clothing made of cotton or other materials that retain water rather than wick it away from the body. Outer layers, including boots, should be waterproof. An extra set of dry clothing to change into if a hunter gets wet is important to keep hypothermia at bay.

SURVIVAL KITS

If the unexpected happens out in the field, a hunter needs to be prepared with a survival kit. Even a minimal kit can be the difference between life or death in some situations. These supplies should guard a hunter against dehydration as well as exposure to cold. A basic first aid kit is also important for treating minor accidents or injuries. With a well-packed kit, a hunter can survive for several days until help arrives.

DID YOU KNOW?

Hunting is one of the nation's safest sports. A person is 105 times more likely to get injured playing tackle football and 25 times more likely to get injured riding a bicycle than hunting.

Some essentials in a first aid kit include bandages and a tourniquet to stop bleeding.

Water filters can be small and lightweight.

There are a few essentials in all kits. One of these items is a water filter. These small, lightweight devices can purify any water. Some of the devices work like straws, and others use chemicals. While stranded in the field, hunters may be unsure whether the water they find is safe to drink. This device can ensure that a hunter has a supply of safe drinking water. Packing a few energy bars along with the water filter will ensure a hunter has enough to drink and eat for several days.

A bivvy bag covers a person's whole body to keep in heat.

Supplies for a makeshift shelter are also key in a survival kit. This can take the form of something quite simple, such as a tarp and ropes. These can be rigged against trees, rock walls, or other natural formations to create a basic shelter. A space blanket can be added to this setup to keep a hunter warm. These thin, metallic blankets take up little room but retain body heat well. A more advanced option than tarps is a bivvy bag. It is a lightweight shelter that comes packed in a small, compact bag. When set up, it can retain up to 90 percent of a hunter's body heat.

Building a fire can also keep a hunter warm as well as alert rescuers to a hunter's location. A survival kit should include fire-building supplies. At the top of the list are matches in a waterproof container and some lightweight tinder. Tinder is a highly flammable material that helps larger pieces of wood catch fire. Dryer lint, cotton balls soaked in petroleum jelly, or small store-bought fire starters are also useful to include.

Hunters can cook food over a fire.

A powerful flashlight can help hunters track a wounded animal at night.

A first aid kit is also a key piece of a survival kit. It should contain enough supplies to treat common injuries in the field. Items include bandages of several sizes, as well as gauze, medical tape, and a tourniquet. Additional supplies include pain relievers, sanitizing wipes, and antibiotic ointment to prevent infections.

Some additional items, if room allows, can make life easier if the unexpected happens. A flashlight or headlamp with extra batteries can make seeing in the dark much easier. A multitool, such as a Swiss army knife, is also useful to include. This compact tool has a variety of useful items contained within it, such as pliers, screwdrivers, scissors, and knives. Finally, a map and compass are smart to bring along in the emergency kit. If a cell phone or GPS device loses service or its battery runs out, these low-tech tools can orient a hunter. Learning local hunting laws, following safety guidelines, and planning for the unexpected while outdoors are essentials in this sport. When those elements are taken care of, hunters can focus on watching wildlife and enjoying their time outdoors.

A multitool can help hunters cut things or open cans. Some even have saws to cut saplings for making a shelter.

GLOSSARY

ammunition
The bullet or shot, together with the other items such as fuses, which are stored in a cartridge and fired from a gun.

camouflage
A pattern of colors and sometimes textures that blend in with the surroundings.

carcass
The dead body of an animal.

cartridge
A case that contains a bullet or shot and an explosive charge.

conservation
The practice of protecting natural resources from destruction.

discharge
To shoot a firearm or arrow.

elevation
The height at which land sits above the sea.

ethical
Relating to a set of moral principles or guidelines.

Global Positioning System (GPS)
A system that uses satellites to determine an exact location.

humane
Acting with compassion and respect toward living things.

hypothermia
A drop in body temperature that can lead to death if untreated.

nocturnal
Active at night.

pelt
A skin with its fur.

silhouette
The dark outline of something against a lighter background.

synthetic
Not natural; made by people through chemical processes.

taxidermist
A person who prepares, stuffs, and mounts animal skins to look lifelike.

terrain
The physical features of an area of land.

tourniquet
A tight bandage or cord used to stop the flow of blood from a vein or artery.

TO LEARN MORE

FURTHER READINGS

Carpenter, Tom. *Hunting*. Abdo, 2020.

Daniels, Patricia. *Mammals*. National Geographic, 2019.

Garcia, Merriam. *The Dog Encyclopedia*. Abdo, 2021.

ONLINE RESOURCES

To learn more about hunting, please visit **abdobooklinks.com** or scan this QR code. These links are routinely monitored and updated to provide the most current information available.

INDEX

PHOTO CREDITS

Cover Photos: Christian Weber/Shutterstock Images, front (bow and arrows); Josh Whitcomb/Shutterstock Images, front (dog); Vika Suh/Shutterstock Images, front (gun); Shutterstock Images, front (target, binoculars, compass, duck call), back (hat); David Schliepp/Shutterstock Images, front (antler); Tom Reichner/Shutterstock Images, front (buck); Wild Media/Shutterstock Images, front (pheasant); Jeffrey B. Banke/Shutterstock Images, front (turkey); WilleeCole Photography/Shutterstock Images, back (boots)
Interior Photos: Csanad Kiss/Shutterstock Images, 1; iStockphoto, 2–3, 15, 57, 89, 103, 114, 122, 126, 153, 173; Steve Oehlenschlager/Shutterstock Images, 4, 22, 33, 47, 54, 55, 99, 104, 120, 124, 131, 142, 155; Universal History Archive/Universal Images Group/Getty Images, 5; Werner Forman/Universal Images Group/Getty Images, 6; Ann Ronan Pictures/Print Collector/Hulton Archive/Getty Images, 7; Shutterstock Images, 8, 10, 12, 20, 26, 31, 38, 39, 41 (top left), 44, 45, 48, 49, 53, 58, 60, 61, 62, 64, 64–65, 66 (top), 66 (bottom), 66–67, 68–69 (top), 68–69 (bottom), 73, 82, 83, 87, 94, 96, 98, 102, 113, 117, 130, 137, 140, 143, 149, 174, 175, 182, 185, 186, 187; Jacob Boomsma/Shutterstock Images, 9; Carolyn Kaster/AP Images, 11, 100; Paul Tessier/Shutterstock Images, 13, 40, 152; Derek Davis/Portland Press Herald/Getty Images, 14; Wild Media/Shutterstock Images, 16; Gutner/SIPA/AP Images, 17; Glenn Young/Shutterstock Images, 18; Annette Shaff/Shutterstock Images, 19; Agnieszka Bacal/Shutterstock Images, 21; Wang LiQiang/Shutterstock Images, 23; Todd Boland/Shutterstock Images, 24; M. Shev/Shutterstock Images, 25; K. Steve Cope/Shutterstock Images, 27, 97; Vaclav Matous/Shutterstock Images, 28; B. G. Smith/Shutterstock Images, 29; Edgar Figueiredo/Shutterstock Images, 30; Jim Cumming/Shutterstock Images, 32–33, 156; Evelyn D. Harrison/Shutterstock Images, 34; Geoffrey Kuchera/Shutterstock Images, 35; Lars Ove Jonsson/Shutterstock Images, 36; Zdena Venclik/Shutterstock Images, 37; Vera Larina/Shutterstock Images, 41 (top right); Chris Rubino/Shutterstock Images, 42; Chase D'animulls/Shutterstock Images, 43; Trapper James/Shutterstock Images, 46; Muro Photographer/Shutterstock Images, 50, 70; Aleks Kend/Shutterstock Images, 51 (top); Nikita Rublev/Shutterstock Images, 51 (bottom); Mykola Senyuk/iStockphoto, 52; Chuyko Sergey/Shutterstock Images, 56; CLP Media/Shutterstock Images, 59, 136; Atlantist Studio/Shutterstock Images, 63; Petr Louzensky/Shutterstock Images, 71; Elena Zakh/Shutterstock Images, 72; Vadim Kulikov/Shutterstock Images, 74; Kordin Viacheslav/Shutterstock Images, 75; Neil Podoll/Shutterstock Images, 76; Alexey Shuklin/Shutterstock Images, 77; Mike LeDray/Shutterstock Images, 78–79; Pavel Rodimov/Alamy, 79; Megan Frost Photography/Shutterstock Images, 80; John Rucosky/The Tribune-Democrat/AP Images, 81; Mitch Kezar/Design Pics/Getty Images, 84; Westend61/Getty Images, 85; Nabil K. Mark/Centre Daily Times/AP Images, 86; Mare Kuliasz/iStockphoto, 88; Raigo Pajula/AFP/Getty Images, 90; Jahi Chikwendiu/The Washington Post/Getty Images, 91; Ricardo Reitmeyer/Shutterstock Images, 92; Keith Srakocic/AP Images, 93; Michael Sean Oleary/Shutterstock Images, 95 (left); Sergei Prokhorov/Shutterstock Images, 95 (right); Tim Johnson/Shutterstock Images, 101; Robert Wedderburn/Shutterstock Images, 105; Dennis Anderson/Star Tribune/Getty Images, 106, 146; Tim Leedy/MediaNews Group/Reading Eagle/Getty Images, 107; Maciej Bledowski/Shutterstock Images, 108; Soru Epotok/Shutterstock Images, 109; Wendy Maeda/The Boston Globe/Getty Images, 110; J. L. Jahn/Shutterstock Images, 111; Anna Hilde/Shutterstock Images, 112; Elena Moroz/Shutterstock Images, 115; Chieko Hara/The Porterville Recorder/AP Images, 116; GoDog Photo/Shutterstock Images, 118; J. Michl/iStockphoto, 119; FogDog Studios/Shutterstock Images, 121; Anna Pozzi/iStockphoto, 123; Robert Nyholm/Shutterstock Images, 125; Taylor Walter/Shutterstock Images, 127; Bridges Photography/Shutterstock Images, 128; Anna Pozzi/Zoophotos/Shutterstock Images, 129; Przemek Iciak/Shutterstock Images, 132; Piotr Krzeslak/Shutterstock Images, 133; L. F. Rabanedo/Shutterstock Images, 134; Zoran Orcik/Shutterstock Images, 135; Linda Freshwaters Arndt/Alamy, 138; Nord Kraft/Shutterstock Images, 139; Remigiusz Gora/Shutterstock Images, 141; John Patriquin/Portland Press Herald/Getty Images, 144; Mark Bugnaski/The Kalamzoo Gazette/AP Images, 145; Jaclyn Vernace/Shutterstock Images, 147, 148; Dan Gleiter/PennLive.com/AP Images, 150; Joe Shearer/The Daily Nonpareil/AP Images, 151; Dirk Lammers/AP Images, 154; Francis G. Mayer/Corbis Historical/VCG/Getty Images, 157; Everett Collection/Shutterstock Images, 158; Everett Collection Historical/Alamy, 159; Brandy McKnight/Shutterstock Images, 160; Jerome A. Pollos/Coeur d'Alene Press/AP Images, 161; Ian Dewar Photography/Shutterstock Images, 162–163; Vlad G/Shutterstock Images, 164; Tony Campbell/Shutterstock Images, 165; Andrii Yarovsky/Shutterstock Images, 166; Michael Macor/The San Francisco Chronicle/Hearst Newspapers/Getty Images, 167; Lawrence Sawyer/iStockphoto, 168; Melanie Stetson Freeman/The Christian Science Monitor/AP Images, 169, 170; Alyson McClaran/The Greeley Tribune/AP Images, 171; Roman Kosolapov/Shutterstock Images, 172; Guy Sagi/Alamy, 176; Jeffrey B. Banke/Shutterstock Images, 177; Edgar G. Biehle/iStockphoto, 178–179; James Whitlock/Shutterstock Images, 180–181; Makasana Photo/Shutterstock Images, 183; Scott Tilley/Alamy, 184

ABDOBOOKS.COM

Published by Abdo Reference, a division of ABDO, PO Box 398166, Minneapolis, Minnesota 55439.

Printed in China

052023
092023

Editor: Marie Pearson
Series Designer: Colleen McLaren
Production Designer: Michael J. Williams

LIBRARY OF CONGRESS CONTROL NUMBER: 2022949206

PUBLISHER'S CATALOGING-IN-PUBLICATION DATA

Names: Conley, Kate, author.
Title: The hunting encyclopedia / by Kate Conley
Description: Minneapolis, Minnesota: Abdo Reference, 2024 | Series: Outdoor encyclopedias | Includes online resources and index.
Identifiers: ISBN 9781098291341 (lib. bdg.) | ISBN 9781098277529 (ebook)
Subjects: LCSH: Hunting--Juvenile literature. | Hunting for sport--Juvenile literature. | Recreational hunting--Juvenile literature. | Encyclopedias and dictionaries--Juvenile literature.
Classification: DDC 796.5--dc23